MAKE THAILAND HOME

A ROADMAP FOR CREATING
A LIFE YOU LOVE IN
THE KINGDOM

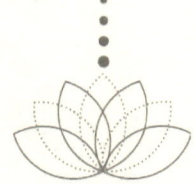

MARK J. FRIEDMAN

To Buppha,
for making our baan Thai possible.

Table of Contents

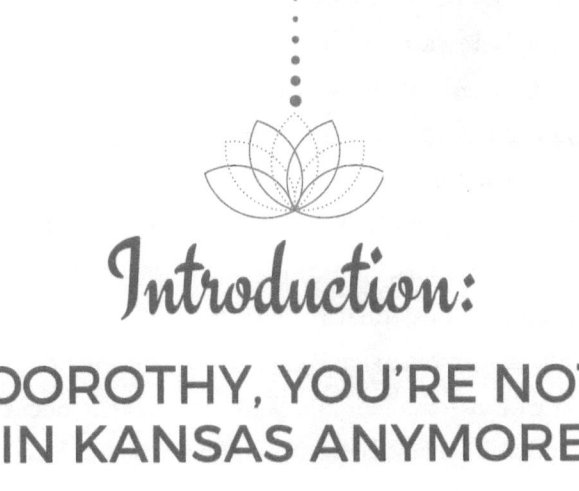

Introduction:

DOROTHY, YOU'RE NOT IN KANSAS ANYMORE

The Journey from Tourist to Resident in Thailand

I imagine you're like many expats I speak with. Those who decide to pack up, cross an ocean or a couple of continents, and take the leap to settle down in Thailand…at least for a while. The stories I hear are remarkably similar. Whether you grew up in rural Alabama, the UK, or New York city, you're the one member of the family with the beat up suitcase getting over jet lag as you plot your next adventure. And while your siblings and cousins are content to stay rooted in their hometowns, you're considering a more permanent move to a new country and culture where people speak an ancient Sanskrit language. In this regard, we expats are kindred spirits, ready to dive into the pool without always knowing how deep or warm the water is. What follows is my attempt to give you a better sense of what relocating to Thailand entails and some lessons learned about how to thrive in this remarkable country.

This may be a blinding glimpse of the obvious, but there is a profound difference between being a visitor and a resident of Thailand. Activities as a traveler are focused on exploration, relaxation, and squeezing as much fun as you can out of your trip as time and finances allow. Making the Kingdom home will include the exploration piece for sure. It will also require interacting with lots of Thai government agencies, negotiating with landlords, figuring out transportation (car or motorbike), finding the best pharmacy to fill prescriptions, and a host of other mundane tasks where signage, customs, and practices may make these chores more or less challenging. While you may expect that getting settled in Thailand will be similar to moving to a new city in your home country, the reality is, things work very differently here. Adjusting to life in Thailand is a process. It won't happen the minute you step off the plane or even within the first few months.

Of course, all of this gets easier over time. And the best shortcut to settling in is listening, really listening, to Thai family and friends or expats who have blazed the trail before you. That's why I've included my personal stories and the wisdom of five other insightful expats who generously share their experiences. My memories are especially focused on those moments when I failed to honor others' advice and how humbling that can be.

I imagine I was a lot like you when I first entertained the idea of moving to Thailand. I was excited for a new adventure and confident I could handle the cultural changes. After all, I am fairly well traveled, with visits to many countries across Europe, the Americas, and Asia under my belt. I had a Thai family and spoke a bit of the language. So, when I first arrived in Thailand as a resident with a new home base, I held my head high, thinking "I got this." But as you'll soon see in Chapter 1, the cultural differences left me feeling disoriented at times, and adjusting to my new home tested my patience and confidence. However, with a willingness to take chances and keeping an open mind, Thailand has taught me a lot. Not just about this country's rich culture and traditions, but also about myself. And now that I've come to terms with not being in Kansas (or LA) anymore, I also discovered that I'm not alone in the challenges I've faced while finding my footing. That's part of the joy of sharing the journey with fellow expats.

Lessons from hundreds of expats and my own experience

During my years living in Thailand, I've spoken with hundreds of expats and newcomers. Many of these conversations have happened through my immigration firm, Baan Thai (meaning Thai home), as I help them strategize about which visa might be most suitable for them.

What's struck me most are the common threads and themes.

There's adjusting to Thai family dynamics, building a house, starting a business, participating in Buddhist ceremonies, learning the Thai language, and navigating life in the city or the hinterlands. This book is my attempt to distill these common experiences and help you peek around the cultural and practical corners I wish I knew about when I first moved here. This is meant to be a roadmap and set appropriate expectations so you can more smoothly adapt to Thai culture. And, you'll be helping me with some good karma if this book helps you not just settle in, but create a life you love in the Kingdom.

How to use this book

This book follows the natural progression most expats take on their journey to Thailand, from toying with the idea of moving abroad to eventually becoming a deeply rooted resident of the Kingdom. As the chapters progress, you'll find guidance on many of the steps it takes to feel like a savvy resident. Each chapter dives into key milestones and considerations, covering everything from the benefits of living in Thailand and committing to the move, to choosing the right visa, picking among the best places to live, and adapting to Thai culture. The final chapter addresses the challenges of living here long term—like buying a house or condo and maintaining your legal status with a solid long-term strategy.

Not every reader, of course, will be at the same stage of making Thailand home. While many of you may be preparing to make the move, others might already be here and looking for visa strategies, home building tips, or ways to deepen their connections to Thai culture. The point is, like a roadmap, not every chapter or part of the book will apply to your journey. So feel free to skip to the sections that speak to your current situation. The book is written in a user-friendly way that makes it easy to find the advice you need for whatever challenge you're facing.

The best way to begin is by getting a glimpse of what that path may look like. That's why I'd like to start by sharing my own story: how I went from a middle-class American kid growing up on both coasts to an expat in Thailand who owns a business, built a home, and—most days—wouldn't trade the move here for anything.

Chapter 1:
WHO

*From Skateboarding Beach Kid
to Business Owner in Thailand*

Before we dive into how best to thrive in the Kingdom, I want to give you a bit of my background. This will give you a better understanding of the perspective for what follows. Frankly, I'm not sure how I ended up with this itch to pack it all up and move to Thailand. My upbringing didn't auger this outcome. We were solidly American middle class. Dad was an aerospace engineer, and mom was a stay at home parent, coach, Girl Scout leader, and cook. We lived in suburbia, attended public schools, and I stayed in the Boy Scouts long enough to become an Eagle Scout.

The seeds that grew into a home and business in Thailand were likely planted when I was growing up in a Jewish neighborhood outside of Baltimore, Maryland. And, yes, I'm still a long suffering Orioles fan. I figured out early on that while my public school closed for Jewish holidays because so few kids showed up, most of the country prayed, worshiped, and celebrated much differently than we did. I also learned from my best friend Dave, who lived in the neighboring gentile community, that Christmas morning was a lot of fun. I ended up crashing the Campbell family's gift opening breakfast for many years.

Then there was the move across the country to Redondo Beach, California, when I was 12. It felt like I landed on a different planet. We lived just a ten minute walk from the beach, and my new neighbors were tanned, long haired, mostly surfers, none of whom were going to Hebrew school. There was also a completely different language. My classmates were "stoked" when the waves were "superior" and most good things were "bitchin." I quickly learned to shed the horn rimmed glasses, grow my hair to my shoulders, and build my own skateboard (yeah kids, there were no skate shops in the late 60s). And after a couple of years in LA County Junior Lifeguards, I was that tanned SoCal kid riding his board down the hill to the beach. Move and adapt, scary and disorienting at first, and then…well, bitchin.

Next came expanding food horizons beyond the familiar meat and potatoes mom labored over every night. I attended a university located in the heart of California's rich farmland. For a college kid on a budget, that meant taking advantage of great Mexican food in small communities like Dixon and Woodland, which were surrounded by corn and tomato fields. Big plates of delicious and affordable beans and rice, and my first foray into spicy with chile rellenos.

Working in LA in the entertainment industry as an agent trainee after university meant meager wages (nearly indentured servitude). But it also gave me the chance to search out delicious, affordable food in the myriad family run restaurants in Korea and Thai Town, East LA, and Little Tokyo. It was my first foray into Japanese food that presented the opportunity to completely embarrass myself. Who knew that the bowl presented after the miso soup was tempura sauce, which I promptly knocked back thinking it was another soup dish…much to the amusement of the wait staff. They were further amazed (maybe horrified) to see me chewing on edamame pods while I wondered how anyone could eat this stringy nonsense. But I soldiered on, willing to dine under the watchful eye and upraised brows of restaurant owners who tried to caution me about spicy salsas and proper noodle slurping. My palate always won out over the risk of too hot, too spicy, and mistaking sauce for soup.

With the sense that I needed greater challenges, I left entertainment for law school. And I loved it, thrived really. By doing something I loved, I was fortunate to have opportunities to advance in my legal career, from great private firms and trial work in Los Angeles and Seattle (yes, I passed a couple of bar exams) to being offered an inhouse position with my largest client. Eventually, I became general counsel to some great US private and public companies, and had the privilege to lead global legal and business development teams.

And while I'm beyond grateful for the opportunities and success over those decades, there is a certain degree of stress that comes with the benefits. This is where I began exploring Buddhism. What drew me at first was the opportunity to practice meditation, not only to calm the mind but to carve out time every day to let go and live firmly in the present. There were also the aspects of universal compassion and tolerance that appealed to a Jewish kid growing up in a predominantly Christian country. Finally, I was drawn to the virtue of patience—

something I sorely lack—which means that I'm merely eons of lifetimes away from becoming an enlightened being.

So, I'm a kid that grew up playing tag in hot and humid summer evenings in Baltimore, enjoying spicy and affordable food during and after college, and practicing Buddhism with the intention of becoming a more patient and compassionate human. Maybe being drawn to Thailand and SE Asia was not such an unexpected outcome after all.

Welcome to Southeast Asia

There is that moment you step off the plane at Suvarnabhumi (Su Wa Na Boom) Airport. After hours of breathing the cool, too dry air of a steel capsule, you're hit with a wave of humidity. And a slightly funky aroma is on the nose.

You trek incredibly long corridors through the airport, get stamped in by a Thai immigration officer, and have your first chance to put your hands together in a wai (pronounced "why") and bow slightly to show respect. You then grab your bags and jump in a green and yellow taxi with your hotel's name and address printed out in Thai. You're not in Kansas anymore, Dorothy.

Then, like the drum solo in *Whiplash*, the energy builds as you wend your way through a blur of glowing lights, temples, and tuk tuks. You step out of the cab, are warmly greeted at reception, and then head off to your first night market. The air is thick and warm, saturated with the aromas of pork grilling on charcoal, the citrusy scent of fresh pineapple, and a hint of lemongrass. In that instant, you have this vague sensation that you've found a home you never knew existed. At the very least, you understand in the marrow of your bones that life will never quite be the same.

The first forays in Southeast Asia can be life changing. It's a deep dive into a world far different from the four square Western culture in which I was raised. Now, I appreciate that for my friends who seek the soft powder of ski resorts or the cafe culture of Europe's great cities, heat and relative chaos is not their cup of tea. Yet for many of us, that first visit to SE Asia is the beginning of a love affair, one that deepens the more you understand the cultures, history, and people. You feel more alive than ever, as if your entire life had been leading up to that moment. You never want to leave. And after that initial trip, I found myself back on the plane to Southeast Asia time and time again.

For over two decades, I explored the region. I drank iced coffee on a tiny stool at an outdoor cafe in Ho Chi Minh City, watching a river of motorbikes stream by. I visited gilded temples along the former French colonial avenues of Luang Prabang, Laos, while the aroma of freshly baked baguettes filled the air. I feasted on a smorgasbord of inexpensive but incredible Indian, Chinese, and Malay eats at outdoor hawker centers, tucked alongside Singapore's polished streets and cosmopolitan skyscrapers. I kept returning to Southeast Asia again and again, and with each visit, I felt more and more like this place was home. Until one day, I met the woman and the family who changed my life.

Falling in love with a local

I'd been visiting Asia personally and professionally so frequently over the years that I started making connections in Thailand. On one visit, an acquaintance introduced me to her cousin, Pha (pronounced Par). We ended up having dinner a few times and, with both of us already being parents, we firmly agreed we had absolutely no interest in anything serious—let alone ever getting married again. On our last night together as I dropped her off in a taxi at her apartment, I felt this catch in my throat. What was this? I tried to brush it off as we exchanged contact details, but I was clearly caught off guard.

Back in LA, Pha and I began emailing each other, and soon enough we were talking on my commute to and from work in Santa Monica. My hour-long morning drive to the office gave her a chance to recount her day, and in the evening I would talk about what happened at work as she greeted the morning. Now, this was before FaceTime. That means I had to use those scratch off prepaid calling cards to cut down on long distance rates. Apparently, we were talking so frequently and I was going through so many calling cards that the lady in Thai Town (in East Hollywood) who sold them to me joked that I must have a Thai girlfriend. "Nope, just a friend," and she smiled knowingly, perhaps having heard this story before.

As our friendship grew, I wanted to meet Pha's family and see Thailand through the eyes of a local farming family. It was this visit in the spring of 2008 that changed everything.

This time in Phetchabun Province, located right in the center of the country, I met her family and got a feel for life in rural Thailand. Pha's village (and now our home) is Ban Phot, literally "Village of Corn." Almost everything we ate on that initial visit was homegrown and cooked over wood charcoal. In one magical moment I watched as Meh Joop (my now mother-in-law) and Old Auntie (known only by her family title) cracked open coconuts with a machete. Both in their late sixties, they then hand grated the coconut meat and wrung it through cheesecloth, producing coconut cream on the first press and coconut milk on the second. That might have been impressive (and tasty) enough, but then they displayed their real culinary prowess. They started a wood fire, brought out a wok, and cooked up the most glorious, spicy, herbaceous green chicken curry (gang keow wan). It was one of the best dishes I had ever had the pleasure of tasting up to that moment, and maybe since. Every element of that dish was fresh and cooked with the skill that only decades of experience can bring. And for Meh Joop and Old Auntie, it was just another day providing sustenance to the family while speaking quietly to one another.

Meh Joop and daughter Pha

A few days later, Pha was driving me around the Province in her extended cab, manual transmission Nissan pickup truck. It was the family's first vehicle other than the ubiquitous motorbikes. June, Pha's 8 year old daughter (and now my lovely daughter), was along for the ride. We spotted a sign for a waterfall I'd read about, and being the adventuresome (and pushy) American, I said, "Let's go!"

Pha was hesitant to drive up a steep, winding mountain road as she'd just got her license. But I insisted, not appreciating just how narrow and challenging the trip would become, especially for a novice driver handling hairpin curves and a stick shift. As we climbed, the truck lurched, stalled, and restarted. About halfway up the mountain, I began to wonder if the truck wasn't up to the task. At this point, being completely stressed out, Pha burst into tears. I reluctantly took over the wheel and was delighted to discover the family truckster had power to spare. We quickly got to within two kilometers of the waterfall where, without signage or warning, we came upon a river where the bridge was being replaced. Pha spoke to the workers, and they insisted we could just drive through the river. "Bai, bai, bai" (go, go, go). Once again, Pha expressed her concerns and, once again, this "can do" American plowed ahead. Hey, we were in a truck, so what possibly could go wrong?

Well, the moment I entered the river, I looked to my right only to see a 10 foot drop down a waterfall. So, I did what I thought any rational idiot driving into a river would do, and I turned to the left away from the drop off. I promptly hit a submerged rock. The truck listed like a sinking boat and June started yelling "Nam, nam, nam" (water, water, water). Sure enough, water was filling the cab and quickly rose to our knees.

As the truck was stuck, I quickly passed Pha and June out the driver's side window to the workers, who were now more than amused by this farang's (foreigner in Thai) inability to drive a straight line. They then brought a skip loader behind the truck to pull me out and started giving me instructions in Thai, which required Pha to wade back into the river to translate. Once the truck was pulled onto the riverbank, I opened my door and, like a bad cartoon, everything that wasn't bolted down in the cab poured out. Here I stood, feeling incredible remorse for not listening to Pha. I had destroyed the one and only family vehicle and, oh yea, nearly drowned Pha's daughter whom I was just getting to know.

Here's the amazing thing. While I kept apologizing, committing to buying a new vehicle on the spot, Pha looked at me and with complete sincerity simply said, "I just want you to be sure you're OK." There was no recrimination or upset about my flooding the family vehicle, which she purchased with 13 years of sweat equity at a shrimp factory. And that's when I realized her kindness and compassion.

The postscript is that the truck ran just fine. After slowly and ever so carefully winding our way back down the mountain, we found a detailing shop right next to our hotel. Within a few hours, the vehicle looked brand new. Oh, and the dent in the bumper from hitting the submerged rock? That was fixed and completely paid for with insurance proceeds. So, in addition to the lesson of really listening to the concerns of your Thai family, staff, or compatriots, it also helps to have a bit of good karma when you plunge into a river.

Later that year, we applied for Pha to come over to the US on a K-1 fiancée visa. We were married within a year of the truck's river baptism. Fourteen years later when we sold the truck, my usually stoic mother-in-law Meh Joop had a good cry when the family's first vehicle was driven away by her new owner.

Moving to Thailand

When Pha moved to the states, our plan was simple. We'd apply for her citizenship, work there until we're ready to retire, and then split our time between Thailand and the US. We bought a nice plot of land in her village one street over from Meh Joop's home, with the idea of building a house there when the time was right (more on building a house in Thailand in Chapter 6). That day came in 2020. The project went from ground breaking to ready-to-move-in within 10 months, and with that, we made our initial move to Thailand.

Living in the house we designed, complete with all the comforts of a Western-style home, made small village life in Phetchabun incredibly comfortable. I was loving the warm nights, tending our garden, and reading in a hammock on the front porch under a ceiling fan. I was truly in the heart and vegetable basket of Thailand and in the center of Southeast Asia. No longer did a halfway-around-the-world flight and jet lag stand between me and the treasures of Thailand. Now, I could spend as much time as I wanted exploring temples, experiencing diverse cultures, and hunting for delicious dishes in night markets—without having to worry about leaving just when I was settling in.

Of course, there were moments of disorientation and missing the flavors and rhythms of the States. Just as Pha took months to adjust to life in Los Angeles, there was a period of shedding my American assumptions and expectations. For instance, when ordering a meal at a local restaurant, dishes would arrive when the cook was able to get them out. Which meant that sometimes desserts preceded entrees and main courses would arrive…whenever. Then there was the daily radio blast from loud speakers in the village, starting precisely every school day at 6:15 a.m. and concluding at 8:00 a.m. with the Thai National Anthem.

And planning anything, ever, just wasn't a thing. The only exception was major events like starting the construction of a house. That could only commence on the day and time our monk deemed auspicious and lucky.

Over time I grew accustomed to the sounds, rhythms, and ways of our new home. Eat what and when food is brought to the table. Do yoga on the front porch to the familiar voices of the radio announcers. And only start a major project when the family tells you that we've received the green light from our monk. Be the leaf in the stream and, as the Buddha teaches, accept and detach from the outcome. Besides, sometimes it's fun to eat dessert first.

Yoga on the front porch

Eventually, I felt immersed in this place. Yes, we made trips to the US to see our lovely family and reconnect with friends. But with each trip I felt more like a visitor and missed our home in Phetchabun. And my family, especially our daughters, were regularly spending time with us in our province and traveling the region. In moments of reflection, it occurred to me that Thailand felt like home. While I enjoyed visiting the US and getting my In-N-Out burger fix, the Kingdom was where we belonged.

So, as with any best laid plan, we planted our roots more deeply in Thailand than we ever anticipated.

My (failed) attempt at being a retiree in a rural Thai village

I know lots of expats who find the life of leisure and exploration to be completely satisfying. One retired US Marine I know (first a client, now a friend) starts his day with a 5 kilometer stroll around Bangkok before grabbing a local breakfast. Then there are the bronze beach denizens practicing yoga on the sand and taking long swims in the Gulf. I get it, and I'm just not that guy. If you're not either, you will find a later chapter that provides advice on how to start a business or work in the Kingdom...if that's what floats your boat.

Initially, it felt great to retire in Thailand. There were many trips to HomePro or Thai Watsadu to outfit and furnish the house. There were ongoing home projects and building additions we realized we needed, such as adding storage and a covered area to eat outside. Then there was the thrill of exploring the country and discovering wonderful places to spend a bit of time—like Nan Province in the northeastern corner of the country, which felt like a throwback to another time.

There was also much to do in our garden, where we cultivate everything from your familiar tomatoes, cucumbers, and carrots to more tropical and local produce, like papayas, bananas, and bird's eye chilies. Equally enjoyable was reading on the front porch in the hammock, which would pleasantly lapse into an afternoon nap.

After several months, the home projects waned and, as things settled in, I began to lose my sense of purpose. I've always imagined a life balanced between quiet moments at home and the thrill of travel. But soon enough, the seams of this plan began to show.

I spent my entire life working and the last 37 years putting in 60-hour weeks as an attorney and part of an executive team. While I loved the quiet country life, things seemed out of balance. It felt like there was a big void that I didn't know how to fill.

At the same time, I didn't love my experience figuring out my long-term visa options in Thailand. When Pha made her way to the States, we were represented by able immigration counsel. There was US centric software to upload our information and populate her visa application, and I engaged a paralegal in Bangkok to help Pha collect documents and prepare for the all important US Embassy interview.

Reflecting on that experience, I expected a similarly structured process when researching my own long-term stay options in Thailand. I knew I could get a visa as the spouse of a Thai national, but I couldn't find someone to provide a roadmap about how to go about that. What's more, there were no software solutions to guide me. I also spoke with folks and plunked around the internet, but was unable to find a resource that clearly explained all my visa choices or the pathway to permanent residency or citizenship that Pha had completed in the US. As I navigated these challenges, I also started looking into how law firms operated here and was surprised to see that local staff were often not rewarded for their efforts. I spoke with Thai friends who worked for expat leaders but, despite their hard work and contributions, were never given the opportunity to become true partners in the business.

So I saw an opportunity to both improve the expat immigration service model and build a firm in the manner of successful US firms. I would do that by making my Thai business compatriots true partners with an ownership stake. And with that, I finally felt a renewed sense of purpose. I formed the Thai limited company Baan Thai Immigration Solutions with Pha and other Thai legal counselors. Thankfully, I had plenty of business experience to get started. I had the privilege of learning about brand building from folks like Howard Schultz of Starbucks while serving as GC at Pinkberry, where his venture capital company, Maveron, was the majority shareholder. I also learned a great deal from Michael Johnson, who was a senior leader at Disney before successfully manning the helm at Herbalife.

It was a challenge to find the right marketing resources and legal talent in a country where my contacts and mentors were 8,000 miles away. There were also significant cultural and legal differences that tested my listening and learning skills. But eventually, and with a few bruises, I came up the learning curve. More on that later.

Baan Thai staff hard at work

Ways I found to connect to Thailand and the expat community

As a new business owner in Thailand, I quickly found that there are lots of opportunities to connect with expats from your home country and around the globe. Most countries have active chambers of commerce with regular social events. Embassies also host parties. For instance, the US Embassy hosted a most welcomed traditional Thanksgiving lunch replete with pumpkin pie.

At one such event, I met an American who told me about his many years as a warden, now Citizen Liaison Volunteer (CLV). This role immediately piqued my interest. Essentially, if a US citizen runs into difficulty or there's a natural disaster, CLVs become the local eyes and ears for the US Embassy or Consulate in Chiang Mai. They can also be a friendly face to someone who is in a stressful legal or health situation and needs to connect with their family. What better way to help people and also make connections with my fellow Americans?

So, as the only American in my village, I thought I might be able to add value to the CLV program. By the way, I know I'm the only US passport holder here because this is a very small village, and our local mayor introduces me as "his American." The program has allowed me to connect with a great group of expats from all over Thailand and the wonderful staff at the Consulate in Chiang Mai. It also offered the chance to get to know local and tourist police officials, as well as municipal and provincial leadership.

The longer I stayed in Thailand, the more I discovered there are lots of ways to make connections and deepen your roots here. There are learning opportunities, such as Thai language, culinary, and Muay Thai academies. There are a host of FaceBook groups that focus on various regions or interests. I randomly belong to three completely unrelated groups: Bangkok Expats, Sandwich Connoisseur, and Isaan Living. You can always make merit at a local Buddhist temple and support the monks' work in their communities. If you're an animal lover, there are charities such as the Soi Dog Foundation. Whatever you contribute will be appreciated; and with most opportunities to give, I find I get more in return.

Lessons learned and mysteries that remain

Moving to any new country can be a humbling experience. As my story illustrates, your attitudes, assumptions, and pace of life back home may not mesh with your new surroundings. It helps to keep an open mind, be ready for the unexpected, and be willing to adapt. In Thailand, it's important to not be too attached to specific outcomes. As you'll see in the coming pages, life here moves at its own pace. People live in the moment, and planning is not a typically practiced skill. If you're too attached to doing things in a certain way or sticking to a schedule, life can quickly become frustrating.

Expats who find the most happiness here tend to adopt a "mai pen rai" (meaning "no worries" in Thai) attitude. They don't get upset when things don't go as planned. They stay curious and make few assumptions. They also practice patience and respect. A smile, a question, and acceptance go a long way in getting assistance from Thais, both for navigating daily life and for understanding what's happening beneath the surface.

As of this writing, I've been visiting Thailand for 25 years, have had family here for 17 years, and have lived here permanently for 5 years. The truth is, I am still learning, and that's a good thing. There are layers of culture and ways of communicating here, developed over millennia, that can take a lifetime to understand. Whether you've vacationed in the Kingdom a few times or have lived here for 20 years, there's always something new to discover about the people, culture, or traditions. That's part of the fun.

EXPAT PERSPECTIVE #1

Army vet and astute influencer

FORREST LEE

CONTENT CREATOR | FORREST LEE

www.forrestleeofficial.com
www.youtube.com/c/ForrestLee
instagram.com/mr.forrestlee
tiktok.com/@mrforrestlee

What is your background, and what brought you to Thailand?

My name is Forrest Lee, and I'm originally from the San Francisco Bay Area in California. I graduated from the University of California, Irvine, and served in the United States Army for close to 6 years. My passion project and fun job is being a Content Creator. As an American expat living in Bangkok, Thailand, I share insights on expat lifestyle, property tours, visa options, and interviews through my YouTube channel.

Inspired by Anthony Bourdain, I first came to Thailand in 2017 as a backpacker, eager to explore my first Southeast Asian country. I had no idea I would fall in love with it so quickly. The captivating blend of Bangkok's vibrant, organized chaos and the warm-hearted friendliness of the Thai people instantly drew me to this wonderful city. Whether you're constantly on the go or prefer a more laid-back lifestyle, there's never a dull moment in this dynamic metropolis.

EXPAT PERSPECTIVE

What was the biggest surprise or something you didn't expect when you relocated here?

One of my biggest and most pleasant surprises after relocating to Thailand was realizing how far kindness, respect, and humility can take you. Approaching situations with a nod, a bow, a smile, and a "thank you" in Thai truly goes a long way. It genuinely pays to be a nice person here, as it should everywhere. Of course, no country is perfect, and Thailand has its share of imperfections. However, despite these, this is the country where I feel I am the most positive and productive version of myself, and where I am eager to contribute to Thai society in any way I can.

What is a bit of wisdom you wish someone had shared with you as you were making Thailand home?

Thailand is a place where you'll encounter all sorts of 'interesting' characters, both local and expat—some wonderful, some a bit like loose cannons. I've certainly had my share of encounters with a diverse range of personalities.

If I could offer one piece of advice, it would be to try not to judge too harshly and to treat everyone with compassion and dignity, even those who seem a bit rough around the edges. Everyone in Thailand has a story, and nobody is perfect. Some are here striving to build a great life, while others might be running from their problems. Regardless of their background, everyone deserves a measure of grace, compassion, and dignity. We're all human, after all, and a little kindness towards one another can make a big difference.

Chapter 2:
WHY

10 Reasons You'll Love Living in Thailand

You find Southeast Asia intriguing and high on your list of possible places to call home, at least for a while. So why Thailand? Some of the countries in the region offer a lower cost of living, great cuisine, and a Buddhist oriented compassion for your fellow sentient beings. So what makes Thailand the most attractive Southeast Asian country for expats from around the world? This chapter is about the "yes and" reasons I chose the Kingdom to call home. For instance, **yes**, the cost of living is great, **and** unlike some neighboring countries, Thailand's well-developed infrastructure makes getting around both the Kingdom and region easy and comfortable. Essentially, you get the best of Southeast Asian energy and additional comforts.

Even if you've visited Thailand and think you know why it's so appealing, I encourage you to read this chapter anyway. Visiting

Thailand as a tourist and living here as an expat are vastly different experiences.

You'll certainly find some well known benefits on this list. However, you may be surprised to learn about the world-class healthcare system and the greater sense of living in the moment that exists here.

So without further ado, here are 10 reasons why I find Thailand an amazing place to live.

1. Thailand is in the epicenter of SE Asia

When it comes to SE Asia, Thailand sits in the heart of the region, and its economy is larger than its four closest neighbors combined. This prime position offers boundless travel and economic opportunities.

From Thailand, you can travel to nearly a dozen countries within a three hour flight or less, including India, Singapore, Cambodia, Indonesia, and Vietnam. Consider for a moment that if you're in some parts of Australia, the US, or Canada, a three hour flight may barely get you out of the country. And even then, your destinations to completely different cultures are limited.

Thailand's central location also makes it an economic hub for the region. Many companies have regional offices in the Kingdom and it is a bustling trade hub and seaport. The country is, for instance, the largest rice and shrimp exporter on the planet. As one of the largest exporters in SE Asia,[1] Thailand is a major trade partner with some of the world's

---

[1] One of the largest exporters. "Thailand's Advantages," Thailand Board of Investment, accessed July 8, 2025.

biggest economies, including the US, Japan, and India. This creates compelling possibilities for entrepreneurs looking to capitalize on Thailand's low labor costs or establish trade connections with their home country. If you'd rather start a small business like I did, you'll also find lots of opportunities. Many expats have successfully opened restaurants, marketing companies, and tech startups.

What's more, Thailand has a long history of friendly relations with Western countries, as well as Japan. You'll find that the familiar Western comforts available here are some of the best in the region, including the private healthcare system and transportation infrastructure. Combine that with deep cultural traditions that have been honored over the centuries (another "yes, and") and it's easy to understand why so many people choose to make Thailand their home.

2. Low cost of living

As mentioned, Thailand's low cost of living is a major draw. Housing, food, and transportation costs are a fraction of what they are in much of the West.

That said, it's not just about price, as other countries in the region like Laos, Vietnam, and Cambodia offer lower costs overall. What really sets Thailand apart is the value for money. The quality you get for so little is remarkable. For only a few hundred dollars a month, you can rent a one bedroom condo with amenities like a swimming pool, gym, and rooftop garden—even in major cities like Bangkok or Chiang Mai. You can dine

---

https://www.boi.go.th/index.php?page=thailand_advantages&language=en#:~:text=TRADE %20SPOTLIGHT,including%20rice%20and%20natural%20rubber

at upscale restaurants for as little as fifty dollars, arrange full time child care for less than a few hundred dollars a month, and order a tailored made suit for less than a hundred dollars. The point is, you can live a life of comfort here for a couple thousand dollars a month. And the value doesn't stop there.

The food, which we'll discuss in more detail shortly, is not only inexpensive but also flavorful, abundant, and available on just about every street corner. You can enjoy a lunch of hot-off-the-grill chicken and sticky rice for a dollar or two. You can feast on the freshest shrimp of your life for as little as $10. Or pull up a plastic chair at a busy street vendor's cart and dive into a bowl of richly flavored noodle soup for a buck.

Gai Yan (grilled chicken in English) in Wichian Buri, Thailand

To give you a better idea of costs as you do a little budget planning, here's what you can expect to pay for the following:

- Furnished Condo or Apartment Rental: $300-$700

- 25-minute taxi ride: $6-$7

- Dining at a Western style restaurant: $6-$20

- 1.5 hour flight from Bangkok to Phuket: $30-$75

- Beer at a restaurant or bar: $1.50-$5

- Reliable mobile phone plan with internet: $6-$15 a month

- Cappuccino, latte, or the like from a local cafe: $1.25-$3

Now, costs vary quite a bit depending on where you decide to live. Prices in our country village in Phetchabun are significantly cheaper compared to accommodations and meals on a popular resort island or the most chic neighborhoods in Central Bangkok. Of course, personal choices matter, like anywhere. Choosing a local coffee purveyor can be a fraction of the cost of an international chain. At bottom, Thailand offers "yes and" choices for the budget conscious and not so budget conscious. That includes everything from the mundane day-to-day expenses of life to finding blissful beach or mountain retreats. I also find expats and Thais are quite willing to share their tips and experiences, so when in doubt…just ask. While we're on the topic of value for money, let's talk about the next big plus of living in Thailand.

3. Great healthcare at a great price

Before we delve into why Thailand's healthcare system is exceptional, let's start with some background. Like many countries, Thailand has both public and private healthcare systems. The public system is free. However, to access it as an expat, you must either be legally employed by a company in Thailand or working for your own company and paying into the system.

If you're from a country that provides public healthcare, the service and quality of Thailand's public system are likely not consistent with what you may have experienced back home. Public hospitals often have long wait times, staff don't typically speak English, and the quality of care can vary. For this reason, I highly recommend purchasing insurance and using the private system, which offers great value for money. Private hospitals in Thailand provide you access to world class medical care for about a third of the cost of most Western countries, and the savings are even more substantial when compared to the US.

Below are the costs of some common healthcare procedures in Thailand:

- Doctor visit for a cold or flu (including medication): $50
- Heart bypass surgery: $13,000
- Hip replacement: $10,600
- Colonoscopy: $830
- MRI: $375
- Daily in hospital stay: $150-$300

Beyond the value, another benefit of Thailand's private hospitals is their concierge style service. Thailand is a top medical tourism destination for a reason. Private hospitals know how to provide exceptional service, often in luxurious environments, and almost everyone speaks English. Many of Bangkok's top hospitals feel more like 5-star hotels than medical facilities. Instead of sharing a room with another patient, as is common in American hospitals, you might get an entire suite to yourself, complete with a separate living space for your family. There are also food courts on site or nearby where you and your friends or family can enjoy a tasty alternative to hospital fare.

Another major perk is the speed at which the healthcare system operates. If you need a specific drug, you can usually swing by a local pharmacy and purchase it without a prescription. Need to see a specialist? You can skip scheduling an appointment or getting a referral through your GP—at most private hospitals, you can walk in and see a specialist within an hour. Finally, if you've ever been shocked or frustrated by a forgotten medical bill that arrived in your mailbox months after your appointment, you won't face that problem in Thailand. You'll typically receive your bill within 30 minutes of your doctor's visit, and it will either be covered by your insurance or you can pay by credit card or bank transfer on the spot.

Healthcare insurance is also affordable, with excellent in-patient coverage available for as little as $40 a month (depending on your age and health). Despite the low costs of medical care in Thailand, I still highly recommend insurance. We'll talk more about that later in Chapter 5, which may be particularly useful for expats coming to Thailand from countries offering a public health system.

4. A big city experience, beachside digs, or quiet country living—you choose

If you've never traveled to SE Asia, you may have an image in your head of serene rice fields and ornate temples. Or you've heard of Bangkok's endless traffic snarls and chaotic electrical wiring. Yes, Bangkok was the fastest growing metropolis in the world for some time. And yes, it took a while for the infrastructure to catch up with all that growth. Yet today, Bangkok is a world-class city that is comparable to major Western metropolises like New York or London. While Thailand's City of Angels may not be quite as polished or orderly as these Western cities (for which I am grateful), you'll likely be surprised by how impressive the infrastructure is.

Bangkok is replete with commercial and residential high rises, has extensive elevated train and subway systems, and is home to some of the grandest shopping malls in the world (Siam Paragon once topped the list of most instagrammable places on the planet).[2] You can find well equipped gyms open 24 hours a day and enjoy grand public parks with myriad sports facilities. Beyond Bangkok, cities like Chiang Mai and Khon Kaen have reliable public bus systems, as well as air-conditioned, Western style condos with access to high speed internet and NetFlix.

The point is, if you want a big city experience similar to what you may have back home, you can get that in Thailand. On the other hand, if you prefer a quieter rural lifestyle, that's also available to you. In our country home and farm in Phetchabun Province, there are no commercial planes in the sky. I can wake up in the morning and pick fresh papaya or

---

[2] Siam Paragon once topped. Karla Cripps, "The most Instagrammed places in 2013," CNN Travel, December 18, 2013. https://edition.cnn.com/travel/article/most-instagrammed-places-2013/index.html

bananas off the trees for breakfast. My wife drives her motorbike down nearly empty streets, surrounded by vast neon green rice fields. Lunch is served in a very down to earth noodle shop run by a fellow villager who has been perfecting her noodle soup for 45 years. There, you can get a delicious meal that you'll rave about for a little over a dollar.

Pi Dang's noodle shop in Ban Phot, Thailand

Lastly, you would be shortchanging yourself if you overlook Thailand's beach towns and islands. For many, this is the dream and why you're considering the Land of Smiles as your home in the first place. You may picture a tropical, palm tree laden lifestyle with crystal clear blue waters and long-tail boats dotting the horizon. Or maybe you imagine settling on an island where you can open a small restaurant, resort, or bar, living a simple life far from the fast-paced stresses of the modern world. In Thailand, you'll have plenty of opportunities to find your beach bliss. Coastal cities like Hua Hin and Pattaya give you many of Bangkok's modern conveniences—international restaurants, condos, and shopping malls—but in a more laid back, beachside setting. Islands like Koh Mak or Koh Lan offer a quieter existence, free from crowds and traffic, with afternoons spent enjoying breathtaking sunsets on serene, sandy shores.

Whether you want a simple life, a view from the beach, or the excitement of Western-style city living, you can find it in Thailand.

5. Laidback lifestyle, vibrant nightlife, and a self care culture

Speaking of the kind of life you want, the lifestyle here is another big draw. Whether you're in a big city, or seaside or rural town, life can move at a slower pace. You can saunter around the streets in shorts and sandals searching for an iced coffee, or grab a plastic seat by a street vendor for your lunch.

When the sun sets, especially in cities like Bangkok and Chiang Mai, the nightlife is diverse and widespread. The rooftop restaurant and bar scene offers the chance to enjoy a drink on a warm night atop a 30 story hotel with stunning views. Elsewhere, you can savor a Thai, Asian, or Western craft beer at a neighborhood restaurant, or keep it simple and have a beer with friends streetside for a couple bucks. If dancing is your thing, Bangkok has plenty of options, be it Khao San road, Nana's popular soi 11, or a more Thai experience at RCA.

The beach party scene is another highlight, especially in southern destinations like Koh Pha Ngan, Samui, and Phuket. Closer to Bangkok, Koh Samet is also known for its beach party vibe. And Pattaya—only a couple of hours away from the Thai capital—might as well be called the Vegas of Thailand with its wild nightlife and glittering resorts.

If all these after hours options leave you needing a deep, cleansing breath, Thailand's wellness offerings are an inherent part of the culture. Like the healthcare system, the value for money is simply incredible. You can easily get a great one-hour foot massage for under $10 almost anywhere in the country, including on almost any street in Bangkok or beach town. A pedicure can also be found for $10, and in our province, the local salon charges 80 THB (about $2.50) for a wash and a blowdry.

Unlike the US, where a trip to the spa or massage parlor is reserved for special occasions, in Thailand, these indulgences can be part of your weekly routine for as little as $40 a month. Pampering is integrated into everyday life. With spas and massage parlors around every corner, it's always within reach when you need a little relaxation.

Pilates and yoga studios, as well as muay Thai academies, can be found in many big cities and beach destinations. Well equipped gyms and personal trainers are available, some open 24 hours. Many larger cities also have bike clubs, and you'll often see groups of cyclists in parks, along highways, or riding in cycling lanes. If you're seeking a more spiritual experience, meditation retreats and opportunities to reside at Buddhist Temples with monks are available around the country.

As you can see, there is a rich variety of wellness activities. The country deeply embraces a self care culture. If you're into wellness, Thailand can be your (inexpensive) ticket to heaven.

6. More freedom, less bureaucracy

If you ever tire of the constant bureaucracy in the West, living in Thailand will feel like a breath of fresh air. Put another way, the nanny state has not made it to the Kingdom. Personal choice and personal responsibility is the norm.

For example, if you have a rash, sprained ankle, or similar ailment, you can typically walk into a pharmacy and get the medication you need without a prescription. I remember early on in our relationship, my wife developed a very itchy rash that we suspected was an allergic reaction (not to me, but some shrimp). We strolled into a local pharmacy and, to my surprise and a bit of trepidation, the pharmacist diagnosed the issue and prescribed medication on the spot. To our relief, it cleared up the problem within hours.

Also, if you're ambling home from a day of toiling at the office and feel like a beer, you can pick one up at your local 7-Eleven and enjoy it on the way—with little to no concern about being hassled by the police or anyone else. Now, there is a law that proscribes alcohol sales in the Kingdom from 2 p.m. to 5 p.m., an odd and sometimes frustrating regulatory scheme. I've heard it's a hangover (every pun intended) from Thailand adopting certain UK alcohol statutes, but regardless, roll with it and plan your beer shopping trip accordingly.

Now, one reason personal reliance is a must is that lawsuits are far less common in Thailand than in many Western countries. People here aren't as quick to sue, with the exception of broaching certain sensitive topics in Thai culture. Even if a suit is brought, there is a long timeline to a final resolution, and courts (and the culture) would prefer that you find an amicable way to settle your differences. While this autonomy does offer a greater sense of freedom, it does come with some trade-offs.

Things you may take for granted in the West—like a hole in the sidewalk, a wet floor clearly being marked with cones, or waiters always asking about food allergies—are rare in Thailand. You need to look out for yourself. In fact, I have a friend who stepped into a closet at a resort looking for beach towels, only to fall into a six-foot hole and break six ribs. Point being, you need to pay attention to your surroundings and take more responsibility for your own safety. Suing someone for your lack of attention to your environment doesn't work here. It's on you.

While fewer rules comes with a few downsides, at the end of the day, you have more personal freedom here and encounter less red tape. Many expats find this greater sense of autonomy to be, on balance, a wonderful benefit of living in Thailand.

7. Food lover's paradise

You're undoubtedly familiar with Thailand's world famous cuisine. However, there are some food traditions and perks you might not expect.

Newcomers to Thailand are often surprised to see that locals rarely eat with chopsticks, and a knife at the table is seldomly used. So how do Thais enjoy their meals? The most common utensils are a fork in the left hand and spoon in the right. Frankly, it's the perfect way to put an array of flavors into a single spoonful of goodness. The fork selects and the spoon delivers. So when you scoop up a bit of rice suffused with an over-easy egg, enjoyed with some marinated pork, you're hit with a succulent punch of salty, sweet, herbaceous and spicy, all in a single bite. How I do anything here other than eat, I'll never know. But what I do know is that asking "have you eaten?" (instead of "how are you?") is the way Thais commonly greet each other, which makes complete sense once you've lived here for a while.

Freshness is also a hallmark of Thai food. Unlike in many Western countries, Thailand has a small farm model, rather than large scale commercial farms. This means ripe fruits and vegetables often go directly from the farm to markets around the country the same day. The fruit is sweet, the vegetables are crisp, and everything is grown for taste, not transport. Freshness and flavor is valued above all else, which makes for vibrant food on the plate. I highly recommend a trip to Talat Thai, just north of Bangkok on Route 1. It's the main vegetable, fruit, and flower market for Bangkok, with daily fresh deliveries of just about everything grown in the Kingdom.

It should be noted that the word for flavorful in Thai is "arroi," and the worst thing you can tell a cook is that their food is "mai arroi," or not flavorful. This may be the reason that when I order food "phet noi," or less spicy, it's usually served a little spicy for Thais, which is just about all the heat I can handle. So to ensure the right level of heat, a tip is to specify the number of Thai chilis you want in your dish. "Prik nueng med" is one chili and "prik song med" is two chilis. Anything beyond that and you're on your own.

The sheer variety of food is amazing. When people think of Thai cuisine, they often think of pad thai or tom yum goong, but there is so much more for your palate to explore. Each region of Thailand has its own specialties. Khao soi noodles and sai ua sausage are famous in the north, as are som tam (papaya salad) in Isaan and yellow curry in the south. The range of fruit on offer can seem endless, including papaya, pineapple, guava, passion fruit, pomegranate, dragon fruit, and so many others. Fresh seafood is widely available—from shrimp to oysters, squid, crab, and fried snapper—all for a fraction of the cost in the West. To compliment the flavors of these dishes, try any of them with nam jim seafood, or seafood sauce, which is a green dipping sauce of garlic, chilies, lime juice, fish sauce, and cilantro.

The foundation for almost every meal is Thailand's world-famous jasmine rice, a fragrant and sweet grain that balances the spicy. Sticky rice, another favorite among locals, is well-known for its pairing with Isaan food or for dessert (mango and sticky rice). With its thicker, chewier texture, it compliments many dishes, particularly skewered meats like grilled pork or chicken. What's more, it's fun to eat with your fingers as you dip the rice into your som tam sauce. For Westerners who aren't used to eating a lot of rice, think of it as the Thai equivalent to the bread of a sandwich. How much better is a chicken parm or capicola when it's in between two slices of crusty bread? The rice in Thailand is sweet and fragrant, and it balances the rich flavors of Thai food, creating the perfect bite.

Of course, after living in Thailand for a while, I do crave some traditional American fare. You'll have no problem finding what calls to you from home, as Western food is widely available almost everywhere. In big cities like Bangkok and Chiang Mai, you'll find a smorgasbord of offerings with authentic restaurants run by expats from France, Italy, Japan, the US, UK, and the Middle East. I've got my go-to New York pizza joint (Chef Bing) and gourmet Mexican fare (Santiaga), and of course a smash burger fave (Stax). There are also plenty of gourmet options, as there are countless Michelin star restaurants with extensive tasting menus, and some are even operated by street vendors (Jay Fai in

Bangkok).[3] The fun in all of this is exploring, which in the Kingdom can be a gloriously endless pursuit.

My favorite pizza with Chef Bing in Bangkok

8. Welcoming and gracious people

Interacting with Thais is like looking into a mirror reflecting your mood and intentions. Happy and grateful travelers in Thailand often recount the genuine warmth of the locals. It's called the Land of Smiles for a reason. Thais are usually smiling and are welcoming to happy foreigners enjoying their vacations. However, once you've lived here a while and the frustrations of everyday life come up from time to time, what you're

---

[3] Jay Fai in Bangkok. Michael Sullivan, "Meet The 74-Year-Old Queen Of Bangkok Street Food Who Netted A Michelin Star," NPR, June 26, 2019.
https://www.npr.org/sections/thesalt/2019/06/26/732529154/meet-the-74-year-old-queen-of-bangkok-street-food-who-netted-a-michelin-star

putting out there can come back to you. For instance, if you're stuck behind a slow moving vehicle, just honk your horn and you'll find yourself proceeding at a glacial pace. Indeed, honking your car horn or any display of frustration, impatience, or anger is never productive.

At its essence, Thailand is a Buddhist country, and the people try to exhibit the religion's ideals of patience and tolerance. If you attempt to speak Thai with a local, they'll be incredibly encouraging, often showering you with compliments on your language skills—even if you can only hold a basic conversation about your family or where you're from. In Thailand, just making the effort is appreciated. You'll find it hard not to smile in these interactions.

Another unique aspect about Thais is their strong sense of community. Neighbors frequently share amongst each other and look out for one another, especially in rural areas. For example, if someone has a mango or banana tree on their property, don't be surprised if your neighbors show up at your door with a freshly picked batch of fruit. In the West, this kind of behavior is common when welcoming new families to a neighborhood, but in Thailand, it continues long after you've moved in.

In line with this community spirit, Thais have a "more the merrier" type of attitude and often invite complete strangers to join their activities. I'll never forget the time I experienced this inclusiveness first hand over a major Thai holiday. I had a friend in town, and on our visit to a local temple, a group of Thais invited us into their circle. Before we knew it (and much to the delight and surprise of my guest and I), we were being taught how to make crafts for the festivities and dancing with the locals. This kind of spontaneous inclusiveness is common in Thailand. Don't be surprised if you're randomly invited to a wedding, a monk ordination ceremony, or a neighborhood soccer game. Thais may even ask you to join them for some after-work beers on the street.

These traits of inclusiveness, community, and friendliness are part of what makes Thai people so approachable. The Buddha also teaches that anger is the manifestation of an intention to harm someone. So, while you're adjusting to a different pace of life and a myriad of other new experiences, patience will be a virtue rewarded by your new Thai community.

9. The comforts of home in exotic Asia

Thailand has a long history of relations with foreign countries. Its formal diplomatic relationship with the US dates back nearly 200 years, and the French, Portuguese, and Dutch had settlements in Ayutthaya as far back as the 1500s and 1600s. The country has never been colonized and tends to stay neutral in most international affairs. In short, Thailand welcomes foreigners and a significant portion of its GDP comes from tourism.

Living here, you'll find a thriving expat community. You'll find Russians and Ukrainians living side by side in Phuket, a Dutch community in Hua Hin, and a large digital nomad presence in Chiang Mai. You'll also find a bustling business community of Australians, Americans, Brits, Canadians, and other internationals in Bangkok, represented by each country's chamber of commerce. Simply put, large expat communities are present in many of the country's bigger cities.

While exploring a new culture is a big part of Thailand's allure, I can speak from experience that you'll eventually miss a sense of connection with your own culture, language, and perspectives. Maybe it's talking about home with a fellow countryman, popping into an old English style pub, or bringing home some Chick-fil-A sauce for your weekend barbecue. In most cases, whatever comforts you long for from back home, you can find them in Thailand.

It's also worth noting that most Thais, particularly in the cities, can speak some English, and quite a few speak it well (though it may be a bit broken). Point being, you can easily live here without speaking Thai. However, I encourage you to learn at least a little, as it can notably improve your life here. We'll talk about that more in Chapter 5.

Among Southeast Asian countries, Thailand arguably offers the best blend of East meets West, especially in Bangkok. There's no other city quite like it in the world. It's a place where street food carts rest in the shade of towering skyscrapers, golden temples meet mega shopping malls, and Muay Thai matches play alongside live soccer in sports bars. In Thailand, you can easily bounce between Western comforts and Asia's exotic experiences as often as you like. So even if you're thousands of miles away from where you grew up, you can still experience a bit of home.

10. A greater sense of happiness (contentment)

While some of us may not like to admit it, Western culture can be very outcome focused. We plan (living in the future) or judge what we do (living in the past), while the present remains just out of mind. We also want results. Whether it's our appearance, wealth, or in my case running a successful business, the end goal matters. In Thailand, the focus and what is valued can be quite different.

Thai people typically aren't preoccupied with the future, the next big opportunity, or planning. Instead, the focus is on the present and how the day presents itself. To illustrate this mindset, let me share an example from my own office in downtown Bangkok. As you know, it's common for us Westerners to ask our colleagues, "What are you doing over the weekend?" However, when I ask my own staff this question come Friday, I often get a peculiar response: "It's not the weekend. I am still working; I'll figure it out when it's the weekend." This mindset embodies the Zen philosophy that says the most important thing you can do right now is the thing directly in front of you. Thais truly live by this mindset. They understand the value of the present moment and won't endlessly chase money or economic opportunities.

In contrast, us Westerners often want bigger, better, or faster. We're hungry for more. Thais, on the other hand, know how to be satisfied. They know when they have enough. They know when they've done enough.

For example, when my wife and I were building our house in the countryside, we decided to install a koi pond. I felt incredibly lucky to find a local koi fish business just a few kilometers from our house to help with the project. Now, small ponds in this tropical sun develop a lot of algae, so I asked some of the shop's employees if they'd be willing to stop by the house from time to time to help clean the pond. I was surprised when they said "no," even after we offered a very generous fee. My wife explained that these folks had enough to enjoy life day-to-day, and it just wasn't worth the hassle. You'd almost never get this type of response from an American business or employees looking to maximize profits or income.

Success as measured by money isn't everything in Thailand. People focus on enjoying life. If you walk around many neighborhoods here at 6 p.m., you'll see Thais sitting with friends on the sidewalk drinking beer, playing games, and kids running around having fun. The streets are bustling with activity in the evenings. Locals know their time is precious and want to make the most of it, and this attitude is bound to rub off on you. That's why you'll find a greater sense of contentment and a more carpe diem type spirit here than in the West. It's one of the most enjoyable aspects of living in Thailand and a refreshing change of pace for many who move here.

EXPAT PERSPECTIVE #2

Insightful mentor and trailblazing entrepreneur

JOANA BUTTON

FOUNDER & CEO | SCALIFY BY SIMPLE SCALABLE SOLUTIONS

www.simplescalablesolutions.com

What is your background, and what brought you to Thailand?

I didn't move to Thailand with a five-year plan. We were only supposed to stay for two. My husband had just been headhunted by Agoda, and after a few heartbreaking years (health issues, burnout, and the stress of building yet another travel tech startup in Sydney) we needed a reset. A break. A breath.

What was the biggest surprise or something you didn't expect when you relocated here?

What started as a pause turned into a pivot. A complete reorientation, not just of career, but of self, of family, and of what really matters.

Thailand has a way of doing that. It slows you down in the best possible way. It strips away the noise, softens the edges, and invites you to listen, especially to yourself. I came here asking big questions: What will my purpose be now? What do I want to build? How can I lead without breaking?

EXPAT PERSPECTIVE

And in the quiet moments, in the chaos of Bangkok traffic, the calm of a temple courtyard, the patience of waiting in line for coffee, or conversations over networking drinks, I began to find answers.

I've spent over two decades helping businesses grow, scale, and transform. I've built teams, platforms, and companies from the ground up. But I've also seen what happens when growth happens without intention: burnout, broken systems, and people left behind. That's what led me to create Scalify, our CRM and business platform. But truthfully, that's just the tool.

What Thailand gave me was the clarity to focus on the why.

Here, I found a community. Through my work with the Australian-Thai Chamber of Commerce, CSR initiatives, and NextGen, I get to mentor young entrepreneurs, collaborate with local leaders, and give back in ways that truly matter. Thailand isn't just a place to do business, it's a place to belong.

What is a bit of wisdom you wish someone had shared with you as you were making Thailand home?

This country has layers. It rewards patience, humility, and genuine connection. Business moves at the speed of trust. Success here isn't about how fast you scale, it's about how deeply you listen, and how respectfully you move. Relationships are everything.

If you're thinking of making Thailand home, my advice is simple: come curious. Ask questions. Learn the culture. Respect the rhythms. Let go of transactional thinking.

EXPAT PERSPECTIVE

What you get in return isn't just opportunity, it's growth from the inside out. You're building something that lasts. Something sustainable. You still get to hustle but you also get to have a life. It's different. But it's purposeful. It has meaning.

Thailand offers something rare: the space to find security and belonging. No, it's not perfect. It doesn't have everything. But it has the right balance. And in the end, I realised... that's exactly what I'd been looking for all along.

Chapter 3:
WHAT

What's Possible?
Your Many Visa Options to Stay in Thailand

After reading the last chapter and learning about all Thailand has to offer, you're ready to pack up your bags and hop on a plane. But maybe you're unsure how long you're able to stay. Should it be an extended holiday, a six month trial, or a more permanent move? As mentioned earlier, visiting Thailand and living in Thailand are far different experiences. Let me reassure you, there's nothing to fear. This chapter will help you come up with a plan.

The good thing about visiting the Kingdom or making Thailand home is you have plenty of options. The government actively encourages tourism, remote working, and welcomes retirees and business investors. Tourism alone accounts for about 10% of Thailand's GDP, and projections suggest this could rise to 30% of GDP by 2030. And, it's estimated that there are about 300,000 Western expatriates living here, including nearly 50,000 Americans. Whether you want to dip your toes in with a quick vacation or immerse yourself in a six-month, year-long or multi-year stay, this chapter outlines the options available for each of these paths. But first, it's important to understand the dynamic nature of Thailand's visa system.

Thailand's evolving visa landscape

In the 20+ years I've been visiting and living in Thailand, the visa landscape has seen continual change. In the past few years alone, Thailand introduced the 5-year Destination Thailand Visa (DTV) for anyone over the age of 20 and the 10-year Long-Term Resident Visa (LTR).

While it's important you're aware of the current visa options, know they may evolve. How much change can we expect?

I doubt any of these visa options will disappear any time soon. That said, qualifications and documentation required by Immigration, the Ministry of Foreign Affairs, or Board of Investment do change frequently. Also be aware that Thai government officials are imbued with discretion on how they implement these programs. For instance, Royal Thai Embassies around the world can have somewhat different financial and paperwork requirements for the DTV program. Also, with the launch of the DTV program and growing number of available visa options, Immigration is increasingly scrutinizing folks making multiple border runs and entering visa-exempt while appearing to stay long term.

At bottom, Thailand will continue to encourage folks from overseas to spend time and money in the Kingdom. So the door will remain open, but you'll need to have the right key in hand to enter the country in a way that aligns with your aspirations. That in turn requires you to have up-to-date information from reliable resources. This could be a friend who has just been through the process, a firm or agency specializing in this work, or a good social network group sharing their experiences. And, while we're talking about resources, the saying "too good to be true" comes to mind. There are many "visa agents" who purport to trade off their relationships with government authorities. They often charge a substantial fee for the privilege of receiving your visa stamp without putting together the paperwork or appearing at Immigration or other government agencies. I've met prospective clients who relinquished their passports, paid the fee, and then had difficulties getting in touch with their agents. While other agents returned the passports with the visa stamps, I would urge abiding by the laws. For one, you're a guest in the Kingdom. Secondly, there's a lurking vulnerability to skirting immigration requirements and a peace of mind and confidence that comes with entering, invited through the front door.

If you're considering a visit or move to Thailand, keep in mind that visa and immigration rules change frequently. To stay informed, feel free to subscribe to my immigration firm's YouTube Channel. You'll get the latest updates on Thai visas and any changes, so you can plan with confidence.

How long do you want to stay in Thailand?

Choosing the right entry path or visa for you will depend on your goals. Are you looking to test the waters and see if Thailand feels like home?

Or have you visited before and know this is where you want to build your life, at least for a while? Start with the end goals in mind. Where do you see yourself in 1, 5, 10, or even 20 years? Is a base in SE Asia part of your vision? If so, are you imagining working here, or using Thailand as your base for exploration? Is Thailand your sanctuary during cold winter months, and you'll be returning to your home country for much of the year? Your answers to these questions will help determine which visa best suits you.

To assist with your decision making, I've broken down your choices into three categories: Try it on, rent it for a while, and home sweet home. Note, the descriptions below provide a general overview of each stay type without getting into too many specifics, as these may change over time. Furthermore, some visas have extensive requirements, which are beyond the scope of this book. If you'd like to dive deeper into the requirements or get advice tailored to your situation, you're welcome to request a free consultation with a Thai lawyer on the immigration team.

Now, without further ado, let's dive in and explore your options.

Try it on: Visit or holiday in Thailand

If you've never visited Thailand but are attracted to its tropical lifestyle, sunshine, low cost of living, and other benefits, you may want to vacation or take an extended holiday here first to see how you like it. Thailand makes doing so incredibly easy, offering straightforward options to almost all nationalities.

Visa exempt: Travelers from 93 countries and territories—including the US, UK, EU, Australia, and Canada, as well as many Asian countries—can visit Thailand without a visa for up to 60 days. How does it work? Simply show up at the border or airport, get a stamp on your passport, and you'll be allowed to enter the country for your vacation. It's also easy to extend your stay for another 30 days. Just submit a simple form at any immigration office, along with a copy of your passport, entry stamp, and a couple of passport photos. The cost is 1900 THB and it will take about an hour of your time.

Now for most folks, a 60 or even 90 day holiday is a luxury and certainly a sufficient amount of time to get a good feel for life and choices of locales in the Kingdom. You can even visit another country in the region and pop back in for another 60 day stay. However, as noted earlier, border hopping as a strategy to stay in Thailand long term is discouraged by Immigration. So if you have a longer or more indefinite stay in mind, read on.

Rent it for awhile: Stay for 6-12 months

If you've visited Thailand before or are adventurous enough to jump straight into a longer, more immersive stay in the Kingdom, you'll be happy to know you have several options. Some of your choices offer multi-year terms. There is also a trade off between expense and convenience as you'll read below. As my spouse points out frequently, we all have different fingerprints. What visa may be right for you is a very personal choice depending on budget, how averse you are to paperwork, how easy you wish to make your stay, and whether you value being able to open a bank account and get fast tracked through the airport.

Destination Thailand Visa (DTV): Launched in July 2024, the DTV visa allows anyone over the age of 20 to work remotely from Thailand (with some restrictions), enroll in cultural immersion courses such as Muay Thai academies or cooking schools, seek medical or wellness treatment, or attend seminars or cultural events. The visa is valid for 5 years and allows you to enter the Kingdom for 180 days at a time. It's an incredibly cost effective option (currently about $400), and you'll need to show you can take care of yourself financially by proving you have the required funds in a bank account. With DTV, you can come and go as you please, and each time you enter the country you're stamped in for another 180 day stay. The visa can also be extended for 180 days at an immigration office within Thailand. Now, you can think of this option as a super tourist visa, so opening a bank account and conducting other business in Thailand is not permitted.

Please note that while DTV and the Privilege visa programs permit working remotely, if you are earning any compensation within Thailand, whether that's as a freelancer or working for a Thai company, you must obtain a work permit from the Department of Labor. Thailand, like most countries, is protective of its workforce, and violating Thai Labor codes can result in being removed and banned from the country.

Education visa: If you'd like to live in Thailand while studying the Thai language, or perhaps take some other college level courses, the Education visa is a good option. While the stay length of this visa has changed a few times over the past decade, it currently allows an initial 90 day stay with the option to extend it for a total stay length of one year. Also, if you want to study Thai and are under the age of 50, and aren't ready to invest in something like the Privilege visa, the ED visa may be your only choice. This is because studying Thai is not an accepted reason for being in Thailand under the DTV program.

Privilege visa: If you want your stay in Thailand to be as effortless as possible while receiving VIP treatment, luxury benefits, and having few immigration obligations, then (as the name connotes) the Privilege visa is for you. It's a multi-entry visa valid anywhere from 5-15 years and offers benefits like a fast track through airport immigration, a 24/7 contact center for support, and a points program offering services focused on your well-being. The visa not only allows remote working, but you can also open a Thai bank account, enter into a long-term property lease, and purchase a vehicle. So, while this is technically another super tourist visa, you can really settle into the Kingdom for the entire term of your Privilege visa.

It's worth noting that Privilege boasts the easiest application process of all the long-stay visas, and if you engage an authorized agent to assist you, it will be at no additional cost to you. The catch is, the visa price tag comes at a higher cost than other options. Fees currently range from 650,000–5,000,000 THB ($20,000–$148,500). However, if time, ease of stay, and truly settling into life in Thailand is your priority, this is a popular option for successful individuals and families. And, if you take into account the cost of living, this visa will likely pencil out in the long run.

Home sweet home: Stay for a year or longer

If you've already spent months in Thailand and love it, or you're certain you'd like to make the Land of Smiles your home, then take comfort in knowing you likely have good long-stay visa choices. Unlike the shorter term options, these visas tend to require more paperwork and can be more challenging to obtain. This is because the Thai government wants to ensure you can support yourself, contribute to the economy, and have a legitimate reason to stay long term.

Retirement visa: If you're 50 or older and would like to enjoy Thailand's easy going lifestyle year round, a Non-Immigrant O Retirement visa is a great option [See note below]. Retirement visas are typically extended for one-year periods, and there is a five year option available requiring more paperwork (e.g. police clearance) and expense. In order to extend for one-year terms, you'll need to have 800,000 THB on deposit in a Thai commercial bank for at least 60 days before you submit your application. To open a Thai bank account, you'll need a long-term visa, which seems like a Catch-22 conundrum, but don't worry. You can apply for a 90-day Non-O visa before you get to Thailand through a Royal Thai Embassy or Consulate and then open the bank account with that visa shortly after you arrive. Now, there are some limitations to this program, as work is not allowed and there is not a path to permanent residency on a Retirement visa.

Note: Non-O, Non-ED, and Non-B are all non-immigrant visa categories designated by Thailand's Ministry of Foreign affairs and simply stand for "Other," "Education," and "Business." The only way to truly immigrate to Thailand is to become a permanent resident or citizen. More on that in Chapter 6.

Marriage/Dependent visa: If you're married to a Thai national or if you have minor Thai children, you're eligible for a Non-Immigrant O Dependent visa—more commonly known as the Marriage visa. This visa allows you to stay in the Kingdom for one year and can be extended annually indefinitely. To extend this visa, you'll need to have 400,000 THB on deposit in a Thai bank account at least 60 days prior to submitting your extension application. And, like the Retirement visa, you can apply for a 90-day Non-O Dependent visa through your home country's Royal Thai Embassy or Consulate, which will allow you to open a Thai bank account and deposit the requisite funds.

Now, unlike a Retirement visa, a Marriage visa provides a path to permanent residency and allows you to obtain a work permit if you're hired by a company in Thailand. This makes sense as the Thai government is acknowledging that you're supporting a Thai family and is placing greater value on that contribution to the Kingdom.

Work visa: Officially known as a Non-Immigrant B visa, a work visa allows you to stay in Thailand as long as you're employed by a company here. The visa, along with a required work permit issued by the Labor Department, is typically arranged through your employer. Arguably the best part about a work visa is that your company's HR department generally handles all of your immigration obligations, meaning you never have to think about 90-day reports, extensions, or visas in general (which we'll discuss in more detail shortly). However, this benefit is a double edged sword. While it gives you a chance to experience life in Thailand without all the immigration hassles, your stay in the Kingdom is attached to your employer. That means if you quit your job or are let go, you lose your visa and have to find an alternative visa or leave Thailand within seven days. You can mitigate this risk if you hold a Non-O Marriage or Wealthy Pensioner LTR visa because those are issued independently of your work status.

A quick note on work related visas if you plan to work or open a business in Thailand. To protect the Thai labor force, employers are required to hire four Thai nationals for every expat holding a Non-B visa. For some industries, such as hospitality or manufacturing, this isn't a big issue. Regardless, if you're planning to use your new business in Thailand as a means to secure a visa, you'll need to take into account these hiring requirements. Now, if you're an employee seeking work opportunities in Thailand, there are a couple visas that give you an edge in getting hired when it comes to the Thai to foreigner ratio requirements. The first is when you are supporting a Thai family while on a Non-O Dependent visa. In this scenario, the expat to Thai ratio drops from 4:1 to 2:1. Secondly is if you hold a digital work permit with an LTR visa. In this case, the Thai to foreigner ratio requirement is removed entirely, eliminating a key hiring barrier and ultimately making you a more attractive candidate to employers.

Long-Term Resident visa (LTR): Introduced in September of 2022, LTR is a 10-year visa intended to attract successful or highly skilled individuals and families to the Kingdom. The benefits include tax exclusions or caps on what you owe, the ability to bring dependents including your spouse, parents and minor children, a digital work permit if you're hired by a Thai company, fast track through the airport, and no need to buy re-entry permits. And for administrative ease, you no longer have to run down to Immigration every year for visa extensions, and your residential reporting is annual—not every 90-days. Clearly, this program has benefits over most other visas, so who qualifies? Here are the four categories:

- Wealthy Pensioner: This is the most popular category for anyone over the age of 50 who can show $80,000 in passive income. Passive income can include pensions (public and private), dividends, interest, and rental income. Private company owners can elect to take their compensation in the form of dividends rather than salary to qualify. The other requirement is having a health insurance policy with coverage of at least $50,000. And even though the title of this category suggests you must be retired, you can obtain a digital work permit if you're offered employment or start a company.

- Wealthy Global Citizen: This is available for any age if you have a total net worth of $1 million and are willing to invest $500,000 in the Kingdom. Investments can include real estate such as condominiums (which are allowed to be owned by expats outright), long-term leases (over 10 years), and building investments. Also included are investments in Thai companies, including a company you form here. Nominally, purchase of Thai government bonds is accepted, but currently there is no practical way for expats to buy these.

- Work From Thailand Professionals: If you're fortunate enough to work for a well established company that will allow you to work from Thailand, this is a visa you should consider. Your company will need to either be publicly traded or have revenue of $50 million over the prior three years. You can be employed by the parent company or a wholly owned subsidiary of the parent, and you'll need to earn at least $80,000 annually.

- Highly Skilled Professional: If you're working or thinking about working in Thailand and have an advanced degree, then you may qualify for the Highly Skilled Professionals category. When launched, these were all STEM-related fields, but this was recently expanded. It now includes, for instance, higher education and vocational instructors. If your application is approved, you'll receive all the benefits of the LTR program (e.g. unlimited dependents can join you) and your income tax rate is capped at 17%.

Why does staying in Thailand become more challenging the longer you stay?

If you've read through all the visa options, you may have noticed that the requirements typically become more challenging the longer the stay length. Why is this?

Before diving into the reasons, I think it's interesting to note that difficulty is a two-way street. While Westerners can easily vacation in Thailand on a Tourist visa or Visa exempt stamp, Thais face far greater challenges when trying to holiday in Western countries. On the other hand, becoming a permanent resident or citizen in the US or UK is much easier for Thais married to Westerners, compared to Westerners achieving the same status in Thailand.

The disparity boils down to each country's unique concerns. Western governments often scrutinize SE Asian visa applicants due to fears of overstays or working, while Thai immigration policies are shaped by concerns of foreigners buying up land and driving up property prices for its citizens. For this reason, and with some exceptions explained later, the only way Westerners can buy property in Thailand is if they become Thai citizens. And the bar of entry to do so is intentionally high. We'll discuss more about the intrinsic value of land in the next chapter and delve into the specifics of permanent residency and citizenship at the end of this book.

Your immigration obligations once you move to Thailand

It's important to know that if you stay in Thailand longer than 90 days, you will likely have ongoing immigration obligations to complete. There are three main ones to be aware of:

- **90-day reports:** For every 90 consecutive days you stay in Thailand, you're required to check in with the government and provide details of your current address. The first report is done in-person at your local immigration office, and thereafter Immigration offers an online reporting system. If you hold an LTR visa, the residential reporting is annual.

- **Visa extensions:** All visas can be extended, which must be done in-person at your local immigration office, and the paperwork is essentially the same as the first time you applied (so it does get to be more routine). Depending on the immigration office and queue, it can take a half-day or longer. If you're extending at the main immigration office in Bangkok at Chaeng Wattana, I recommend getting there early or try booking an appointment.

- **Re-entry permits:** If you plan to leave Thailand and return on the same visa, you'll need to get a re-entry permit before departing. Re-entry permits can be obtained at your local government office or the airport. If you fail to get your re-entry permit, you essentially lose your visa when you return to the Kingdom. I know from personal experience. I had that Homer Simpson moment halfway across the Pacific, "Doh," when I realized I forgot to purchase one before departing from Suvarnabhumi Airport. I recommend buying the re-entry permit every time you go to Immigration to extend your visa and not risk blowing up the visa you worked so hard to obtain.

For many expats, 90-day reports and annual extensions become a source of irritation. Visiting a government office can be time consuming, and remembering to file a 90-day report and keeping track of how much time you spend in the Kingdom can feel like a recurring annoyance.

Just like I mentioned in the last chapter, the expats who thrive in Thailand are often those who accept these immigration duties as part of life here, and be that leaf in the stream. However, if you dread completing them, you have options. This is where understanding all of the visa programs and putting in place a long-term plan, including a path to permanent residency, helps to avoid the particular frustrations that may get under your skin over the long term.

Does your immigration status match your ties and aspirations?

When you first arrive in Thailand, you may lack a clear plan. As mentioned, maybe you come here to vacation or test living in the Kingdom. That's great at first. But if you decide to stay here on a more permanent basis, it's important to periodically check in with yourself. Does your visa status align with your financial, social, and emotional ties to Thailand? Does it fit your long-term vision for staying here? Let me illustrate why this is important with a common scenario many expats eventually find themselves in.

Let's say you come to Thailand for nine months and fall in love with the country. You decide to stay permanently, get a job in Bangkok, perhaps buy a condo, grow a circle of friends, and even start a romantic relationship. In other words, you build a life here. Working for a local company in Thailand is one of the easiest ways to stay here long term.

Outside of Thai citizenship, it's the only option that eliminates immigration responsibilities entirely—or rather, it passes them on to the HR department of your employer. That means HR takes care of your visa extensions, 90-day reports, and even your re-entry permits. But what happens if you leave your job or are let go?

It doesn't matter how many years you've been in Thailand. You could be here for a decade, but if you leave your job, your visa is canceled and you're forced to leave the country or find an alternative way to stay within seven days. Talk about a stressful experience. Suddenly, in a place you considered home, you're scrambling as you race to figure out your next move. Get another job? Leave and come back on a tourist visa exempt and then figure it out? Given the short timeline, your options are limited.

This is why periodically thinking about your future plans, assessing your visa status, and having a long-term strategy is essential for your peace of mind. You don't want to find yourself in a situation where you feel like you're being uprooted just because there was a change in your job or family circumstances. With a little planning, you can go a long way in mitigating or eliminating this risk. For instance, while still employed, you may become eligible to apply for an LTR visa or permanent residency. Either option can provide you the flexibility to stay in Thailand regardless of your employment status. You'll have the breathing room and freedom to make the best choices for your life—not dictated by visa limitations.

Another advantage of visa planning is the ability to choose stay options that minimize immigration obligations. If you dread 90-day reporting, re-entry permits, and annual extensions, there are alternatives. For example, with permanent residency, you'll never have to deal with extensions or 90-day reports. And with LTR, your re-entry permits are included, your extension occurs after 5 years, and you are only required to report once a year, rather than every 90 days. With the Privilege program, you never have to extend over the entire 5, 10 or 15 year term. And if you're in Bangkok, the Privilege staff takes care of your 90-day reporting.

On the other hand, if you don't mind handling the immigration requirements and only plan to stay in Thailand for a few years, a Non-O Retirement or Marriage visa might be your best fit.

As you can see, your preferences and aspirations for living in Thailand play a vital role in determining your best long-stay option. Aligning your visa or legal status with this vision ensures (as we've seen with many expats we've worked with) you'll have a better, happier experience in the Land of Smiles. You'll enjoy the peace of mind that comes with knowing your future here is stable and that leaving will be on your terms—not because a visa forces you to make a hasty decision.

Tips on productive interactions with officialdom and service providers

As you can imagine, dealing with banks, police, and locals in Thailand will be quite different from back home. It's also unavoidable. If you move here, you'll eventually need to open a bank account, lease a condo or apartment, and interact with government staffers, including Immigration, the Department of Land Transportation for driving licenses, or your local amphoe or district office. How can you ensure these interactions go as smoothly as possible? Let's take a look.

Immigration

If you've never lived in a foreign country before, visiting immigration can be an eye opening experience. You'll typically find hundreds of people waiting to see a couple dozen hard working immigration officers—making the environment crowded, noisy, and a bit chaotic. For your visit to go smoothly, it's important to show up with an attitude of empathy, respect, and patience.

Empathy with immigration staff is understanding that they will discharge their duties to 50, 75, or more applicants each day. What's more, those applicants will approach the counter speaking a variety of languages and accents. Some will be well prepared or represented by an experienced legal counselor or agent. Others will think they know what to do, but were failed by outdated information they found online. So if the crowds and chaos make you a bit anxious, imagine working in that environment every day for years.

Showing respect means dressing for success and making a good first impression. Leave behind the tank tops and flip flops for your next visit to the beach, and wear long pants, a collared shirt, and closed toe shoes. Look around and you'll see almost all Thais dressed this way. It also means arriving at the desk with organized paperwork neatly compiled in a file folder, communicating to the officer that you put thought and effort into the visit. Knowing your stuff and having consulted with a knowledgeable resource, such as a friend who has been through the same process many times, will make you stand out as someone who is making the officer's job that day easier, not harder. And finally, a smile, a "Sawaadee," and hands together in a wai will directly communicate your respect for the process and staff.

Finally, practice patience. The officer is the only person who can decide the outcome of your application. He or she has not only the authority but the discretion to approve or deny it. Think of a request for additional documents or photographs as a learning opportunity. And know that any signs of frustration or impatience will work against you. Staying cool, smiling, and returning to the counter with the additional information or documentation will pay dividends and get your matter to the finish line.

Police

You'll likely have fewer interactions with the police in Thailand than in your home country. For example, it's pretty rare to be pulled over here. However, if you are, follow the same guidelines as you would with immigration. Now obviously, you can't control how you're dressed when you get pulled over, but you can still show the officer respect. Smile, wai, and remain calm. And under no circumstances should you get angry or impatient. As mentioned in the last chapter, Thais tend to reflect your mood and intentions. The last thing you want is to deal with an irritated Thai police officer who has the authority to hit you with a hefty fine. So stay calm.

Also, if you respect the laws here to begin with, you'll set yourself up for smoother interactions with the police. You can get an international driver's license before leaving your home country. This makes it easier to apply for a Thai driver's license when you arrive here. As long as you have a driver's license in your home country, obtaining one in Thailand isn't difficult and shouldn't take more than a half day or so. Watch the required video at home (there's a link on the Land Transportation Department's website) and print out the certification. As with most government agencies, arrive early with your passport and pink Thai ID if you have one, and you'll be run through a quick peripheral vision and braking reaction test. That's it. However, if you're in the provinces, it helps to know how to say red, yellow, and green in Thai (si dang, si luang, si keow), as you'll be asked to identify colors in the vision test.

Also, keep your vehicle registrations up to date as there are the occasional checkpoints in the provinces to verify compliance. You can tell when you're approaching one of these because a long line of non compliant trucks and cars will be parked on the roadside. They're waiting for the police manning the checkpoint to break for lunch or pack it in for the day.

If you do get stopped by the police, be prepared to possibly pay a small fine on the spot. It's common for officers to find a technicality, such as a paperwork issue or an expired license. The fee shouldn't be much. Likely a few hundred baht, and then you can go on your way. As we've discussed, accepting that Thailand operates differently from your home country will make these interactions much less stressful.

Banks

The banking system in Thailand is likely a bit different from that of your home country. Traditional checking and savings accounts don't function in the same way here. While the most common account is in fact a savings account, it works more like a commercial account rather than a traditional interest-bearing savings account.

When it comes to paying for goods and services, credit cards are not easily available in Thailand. It's a good idea to maintain your overseas credit cards and an overseas bank account if you can, as many foreign credit cards are accepted at most hotels, department stores, and the like. Otherwise, many people pay in cash, and ATMs are everywhere. However, paying by scanning a QR code is incredibly popular—even among street food vendors. It's quick, easy and efficient, but you'll need a Thai bank account.

If you come here as a tourist visa exempt or even as of this writing with a multi-year DTV visa, opening a bank account is not allowed. Generally, you'll need to be on a long-term visa to qualify, but this can include 90-day Non-O and Non-B visas, which can later be extended to one-year terms. It's also worth noting that not many bank staff will speak English (even in Bangkok) and some of the required forms to fill out may be in Thai. Having a Thai friend, family member, or counselor assist you can make the process much easier. If you'd like more detailed instructions on opening a bank account here, you can check out this article The Ultimate Guide to Opening a Thai Bank Account for Expats.[4]

Landlords

When renting a condo or apartment in Thailand, you'll typically need to pay three months up front: two for the security deposit and one for the first month's rent. You should never pay your entire lease up front as your circumstances could change or you may discover unpleasant surprises in the building (like lots of noise, repairs, or a bad internet connection) that may make you want to break the lease.

---

[4] The Ultimate Guide. Mark Friedman, "The Ultimate Guide to Opening a Thai Bank Account for Expats," Baan Thai Immigrations Solutions, June 13, 2022. https://btisolutions.co/how-to-open-thai-bank-account/

It's also important to find a landlord who is approachable, responsive, and cooperative. Why? Your landlord plays a role in your immigration responsibilities. For example, they're required to file a TM30 form and you may need specific documents from them for visa extensions. While completing these tasks is usually not an issue for landlords, it's still important to discuss these matters before signing your lease.

A final note is that most landlords will include furnishings, such as beds, coffee tables, and televisions. So there's no need to worry about shipping bulky items from your home country or finding a furniture store. Now, things are a bit different when building a home or buying a condo, but don't worry as furniture stores are abundant. Plus, you can look forward to hours of fun assembling your purchases from IKEA, which are present in the major cities.

Service providers and contractors

Finding reputable service providers in Thailand can be more challenging than in Western countries. Unlike back home, there's no app like Angie's List where you can get reviews and insights into a contractor's performance and reputation. This means you'll need to do more due diligence when selecting a service provider. If they do a terrible job or take your money and run, there is no real recourse.

The best way to mitigate this risk is through referrals. Ask your friends, neighbors, or family for recommendations. Once you find a good service provider, nurture that relationship. In Thailand, service interactions are often very transactional. Even if you go for a health check up or teeth cleaning, you may see a different doctor or dentist each time. So with service providers, the key is to build a long-term relationship and treat them like family. Oh, and always pay fairly and pay on time.

A strong relationship with a service provider can be invaluable in emergencies. For example, if our water pump broke at home, my wife could call our service provider K. Rangsee and he'd be at our front door within an hour. Without that relationship, we'd have to find someone on the fly, potentially waiting days for the repair while also taking the risk of hiring an untested provider.

So, do yourself a favor, and make friends with your trusted service providers. Be their most reliable customer when it comes time to make payments. And yes, for lunch pick up those extra chicken or noodle dishes for the crew when at the market, and they'll be there in a pinch when you need them most.

EXPAT PERSPECTIVE #3

Exchange student to digital marketing leader

JAN ROHWEDER
CEO & FOUNDER | MARKETING BEAR

www.marketingbear.com

What is your background, and what brought you to Thailand?

My journey to Thailand was quite a happy accident. I had initially planned on an exchange semester in the United States, but my best friend, who is half-Thai, convinced me to join him in Thailand instead.

My background is in marketing, and after my exchange semester, I started with an internship at a local PR and marketing agency, which evolved into a full-time role. After a few years, with the encouragement of my former bosses, I founded my own digital marketing agency, Marketing Bear, in late 2013. We're a data-driven agency in Bangkok, and I also have the privilege of serving as a director of the Australian-Thai Chamber of Commerce.

EXPAT PERSPECTIVE

What was the biggest surprise or something you didn't expect when you relocated here?

While there have been countless big surprises since moving here, I'll pick one of the very first ones I experienced when arriving in Bangkok. This was the 24/7 nature of life, which was a stark contrast to my experience in Germany. In Germany, I was used to a structured Monday-to-Friday schedule, with stores closing early in the evenings and on Sundays.

In Thailand, however, there's almost no difference between the weekdays, and the energy continues around the clock. You can find buzzing restaurants, co-working spaces, and even gyms open in the middle of the night. From a business perspective, this lack of limitation on operating hours is a great opportunity, as it allows you to attract more customers. The city's non-stop energy can be quite addictive once you adjust.

What is a bit of wisdom you wish someone had shared with you as you were making Thailand home?

If I could give my less-experienced expat self one piece of wisdom, it would be to engage with the local business community from the very beginning. I mistakenly started out by focusing only on clients in Europe and the US, believing that was where the larger budgets were. It was a complete misconception. There is a significant demand for high-quality services right here in Thailand, and I learned that overlooking the local market means missing out on great opportunities.

Chapter 4:
WHERE

Where to settle down:
Big city, beach town, mountain village, or farm country

With your passport and visa in hand, you are one step closer to making your dream of Thailand a reality. You can almost taste the sweet papaya and mango, and breathe in deeply the fragrance of tropical flowers. You're excited…perhaps feeling like Red, Morgan Freeman's character in *The Shawshank Redemption*, crossing the border into Mexico as a free man. What will your new life look like? Perhaps you envision days of endless sunshine, beaches, and sunsets over the water. Or living on the 37th floor of a condo with all the amenities along with sweeping views of Bangkok's skyline. Before committing to a location, know that Thailand offers more than beaches and Bangkok.

Just as we all have a unique set of fingerprints, the decision of where to settle and what type of accommodation you prefer is deeply personal.

For instance, if you're a frequent overseas traveler, you'll likely want relatively easy train or taxi access to a major international airport, such as Bangkok's Suvarnabumi or Chiang Mai International Airport. If you crave the constant, energetic hum of a major city, there are at least a few urban areas in which to thrive. There are a variety of islands and beach locales to consider, from the sublimely quiet to the full on Waikiki resorts and shopping meccas. And, beyond its famous coastlines and capital, the Kingdom boasts a diverse range of other landscapes and lifestyles. With a little exploring, you'll find mountainous regions surrounded by national forests for trekking, a village with a distinct hippie vibe, and cities and towns with scarcely an expat in sight.

As we learn in life, sometimes our choices are not exclusively our own. If you're a parent of school age children, you will likely be considering neighborhoods where your kids are enrolled. Which, by the way, offer some very nice choices as you won't be the only expat in the neighborhood. Of course, the same is true if you're working in the Kingdom. Commuting times can either be relatively short or brutally long, especially if you're driving in Bangkok during rush hours. So strategies around access to public transportation and toll roads are advised. And as you're going through this exercise, it's also a good idea to ask around about conditions during the rainy season. Some areas of every city and town tend to become impassable during downpours, while others remain navigable.

In the following pages, you'll learn about the five main regions of Thailand where expats tend to live. Because Bangkok has a population rivaling most Scandinavian countries and a sprawling and diverse series of neighborhoods, I've included it as a region of its own. We'll also cover Northern, Southern, and Central Thailand, as well as Isaan, highlighting the sorts of expats that may be best suited for each area. That said, this chapter isn't a comprehensive guide. We won't be getting into Western Thailand or places like Kanchanaburi and Mae Hong Son, and we'll only briefly touch on Isaan. Regardless, I encourage you to explore not only the places covered here but also those that aren't. Thailand is far more diverse than many people realize. With some research or social media outreach, you're likely to find an expat willing to share their experiences in almost all these locales.

The moving to Thailand checklist: What to know before you go

Before we explore Thailand's regions and cities, let's go over a few important things to know before packing your bags. Moving to Thailand isn't your typical change of address. Remember, you're not only moving to a new country but also adapting to a new culture and climate. So, here are some things to keep in mind.

Do a short lease to start: Many of the cities we'll cover have neighborhoods, and life can vary dramatically from one to the next. In Bangkok, for example, you could enjoy a glamorous high-rise lifestyle downtown, opt for a quieter townhouse by the river, or even settle into a country-style home on the city's more rural outskirts. You may not find your ideal neighborhood (or even city) straight away. That's why I recommend starting with a one-year lease for an apartment or condo. It gives you time to see if the area suits your lifestyle without committing long term. By the way, this is the minimum lease term for a Non-O Retirement visa. The government requires this to be sure you'll have adequate housing during the entire one-year visa term.

Know that appearances are often deceiving: In Thailand, what often looks beautiful on the surface may reveal some unexpected downsides later. Your dream townhome could be in the vicinity of a pack of aggressive soi dogs, or your neighbor might own a rooster that starts crowing at 3 a.m. This is why it's important to begin with a one-year lease. You'll have time to see not just the upsides but also the warts before making a long-term commitment.

Leave the furniture behind: As mentioned in the last chapter, most condos and apartments in Thailand come fully furnished, and buying new furniture is both easy and affordable. If you can't find an IKEA near you, HomePro (similar to IKEA) and other furniture stores can be found throughout the country. Shipping your purchases within Thailand is much less expensive than you've experienced. You can easily ship that IKEA bed and mattress anywhere—including to remote villages, which I learned from personal experience. And yes, the IKEA Swedish meatballs are a delicious treat after you're done shopping.

While I do generally suggest leaving the furniture behind, there are two exceptions to this rule of thumb. If you're married to a returning Thai national, he or she can make a shipment into Thailand duty free, which can be a big savings. Also, if you're arriving for a business assignment with a Non-B visa, customs duties may be waived. So if you think you'll miss your favorite large screen TV or sleeping in your own bed, then by all means ship those items. All the better if your company is paying the freight.

Understand the difference in leasing condos or apartments: Renting in Thailand works a bit differently than you may be used to, as you'll often have more opportunities to lease a condo than an apartment. What's the difference? When you rent an apartment, the entire building is owned by a single landlord who rents units to all the tenants. In contrast, each condo unit is individually owned, meaning you'll lease directly from that specific owner. Another difference to be aware of is internet access. Apartments often have a shared internet connection for an entire floor (similar to hotel Wi-Fi), while condos allow you to set up your own dedicated internet line. Shared apartment Wi-Fi can be slow, especially if dozens of people are using it at once. So if you need a strong connection for work or other reasons, discuss your options with the landlord before moving in. For more tips on leasing, see the Landlords section at the end of Chapter 3.

Bring your best friend: Thailand is pet friendly and bringing cats and almost all types of dogs is a relatively simple process that takes just a bit of planning. There are vaccinations to document and some forms to have in hand. However, unlike other jurisdictions, if your pet is vaccinated and healthy, there is no quarantine period. Here's a link to the Bring Your Pet to Thailand Checklist,[5] a guide that explains this in a bit more detail.

---

[5] Bring Your Pet to Thailand Checklist. Mark Friedman, "Bring Your Pet to Thailand Checklist," Baan Thai Immigrations Solutions, accessed July 14, 2025. https://btisolutions.co/lp/bring-your-pet-to-thailand-checklist/

Pi Boy and Nong Ann

Kuhn Paw on his trusty bike

Noodle soup time in Ban Phot

Pha and our cat Cha Nom

Vegetable vendors at Talat Ban Phot

The 5 most popular regions of Thailand for expats

You're finally at that pivotal moment in your journey: where are you going to live? Below, we'll cover the popular cities and towns in Thailand's five main regions for expats, and I'll help you make an informed decision about where to explore and what location may be right for you.

Bangkok

Often ranked as the most visited city in the world, Bangkok[6] is home to 11.5 million people. It is a vast metropolis of striking contrasts. A city where towering skyscrapers and sprawling mass transit networks coexist with traditional riverside bungalows and neighborhoods clustered around international schools where kids go trick or treating every October. You'll find just about everything here. As mentioned in Chapter 2, Bangkok offers a melting pot of international cuisines and a vibrant rooftop bar and nightlife scene. The city is also home to some truly spectacular parks, including Benjakitti and Lumphini, both over 100 acres and offering a peaceful retreat from the urban buzz.

Like many major cities, Bangkok has hundreds of neighborhoods that each have their own distinct vibe. There's the Japanese area of Thong Lor with its traditional Japanese dining spots. The upscale Ari has a fantastic restaurant scene and plenty of greenery for nature lovers. And there's the hipster riverside neighborhood of Talad Noi with its trendy

---

[6] Often ranked as the most visited city. Alexandra Talty, "Bangkok Is The Most Visited City In The World...Again," Forbes, Sep 04, 2019.
https://www.forbes.com/sites/alexandratalty/2019/09/04/bangkok-is-the-most-visited-city-in-the-world-again/

cafés and colorful street art. Despite Bangkok's bustling core, the city can become surprisingly rural as you get closer to its outskirts. Sometimes so much that it's as if you're stepping into a quiet Thai village far from the chaos of city life. This variety of experiences makes Bangkok's endless side streets (sois), diverse restaurants, and countless shops a place you could spend a lifetime exploring. It's worth taking the time to discover which neighborhood best suits your lifestyle.

Of course, Bangkok has its drawbacks. The city regularly ranks among the worst in the world for air pollution in the early part of the year. It can also feel hotter than other parts of Thailand due to the dense concentration of cars, concrete, and high-rise buildings. Temperatures regularly hover around 90 (32 Celsius) year round.

As a major metropolis, Bangkok can be noisier and more chaotic than many Western cities, largely because noise pollution laws are less strict and traffic rules aren't always enforced. Don't be surprised if you see motorbikes driving on the sidewalk.

Who is Bangkok best suited for? Like most major, densely populated cities, folks make Bangkok home for a wide variety of reasons. If you're a big city person, want to be part of a large expat community, and need to be close to the airport due to frequent travel, Bangkok is an excellent choice. If healthcare is a priority, the city has the largest concentration of first class hospitals and clinics. And if you're a parent, the international school choices will be greater than elsewhere in the Kingdom. However, there certainly are good schools in almost every major expat community, so let's move further afield.

Central Thailand

If you draw a circle around the central part of the country, you'll cover everything from popular beachside cities and towns, verdant farmland, and spectacular mountain enclaves. Our home province, Phetchabun and its neighboring provinces, are typically home to expats with Thai families. Once you get closer to the beach in places like Pattaya, Rayong and Hua Hin, the expat communities are quite robust, and so are the corresponding housing, food, and entertainment options. Here are some of the most popular cities in Central Thailand for expats.

Pattaya

Pattaya has a debaucherous reputation, but don't let that turn you off from considering Bangkok's beachside neighbor. While it's true the city's Walking Street does have the "trade," like most cities with red light districts, it's mostly confined to an area you can choose to avoid. Many expats who choose to live in Pattaya and surrounding communities simply enjoy everything else the city offers.

Along with Phuket, Pattaya is one of Thailand's most developed beach towns. Much like Bangkok, it offers diverse, international cuisines and great seafood, as well as malls, markets, and plenty of activities geared toward tourists and locals alike. You'll find everything from craft breweries to water parks and even a wine vineyard. Surprisingly, the water quality is better than many expect. And venture a little farther to nearby Koh Lan (just a short ferry ride away), and you'll find yourself immersed in island life with even cleaner water and a more laid back atmosphere.

Thanks to Pattaya's popularity among expats, the city has an abundance of affordable rental options—often at a fraction of what you'd pay in the US for beach living. This makes it an attractive destination for those seeking both comfort and value. If you travel often, you'll be glad to know that Pattaya is only about an hour and 20 minutes from Suvarnabhumi Airport. What's more, the beach town is well-connected to Bangkok. There are regular minivans and buses running between the two cities, making trips to the capital fairly quick and convenient.

Pattaya is located in Chonburi Province, and if you explore beyond the tourist hub of the city, you'll quickly discover quieter beachfront communities set in more rural surroundings, such as Bang Saan and Rayong. The vibe is much more low key, the traffic is lighter, and you'll still enjoy beachside living close to Bangkok.

Who is Pattaya best suited for? If you love the beach, want easy access to Bangkok and the airport, and wish to be around a large expat community, you'll likely enjoy living in Pattaya or its surrounding areas.

Other Destinations in Central Thailand

While not all expats want to live in a big city, many still prefer to stay in proximity to one for convenience and access to medical care. If that sounds like you, consider these locales, including beachside and rural options, each offering a lifestyle that you may find to be the right fit.

Hua Hin

If you're looking for a more laid-back beach town, Hua Hin is worth considering. Located about two and a half hours from Bangkok, it offers a slower pace of life while still providing many conveniences. Like Bangkok and Pattaya, Hua Hin has a sizable expat community, a wide variety of restaurants, and good healthcare options—though the city isn't as developed as Pattaya. It also offers a number of reasonably priced pool villa single family homes, as well as large condo high rises in Cha Am, just north of the city.

Hua Hin is also a haven for cyclists, with a surprising number of well marked bike paths to explore. And being a coastal town, it's known for its outstanding seafood. Unlike Pattaya, Hua Hin attracts fewer rowdy tourists and more families, offering a more peaceful vibe. Be mindful that the water in Hua Hin isn't as clear as in Pattaya (you could even go as far as describing it as murky at some beaches). While it's still great for swimming, those seeking crystal-clear waters for snorkeling or diving should look elsewhere. South of Hua Hin there are beach camping opportunities and raised walks and boat tours through the mangrove swamps.

Hua Hin is also the traditional summer retreat for the Royal Family. There is a wonderful seaside palace, constructed in 1924 under the direction of King Rama VI, that blends the best of Thai and Western architecture. Also worth visiting is the Hua Hin Artist Village with its eclectic collection of modern and traditional art, perfect for finding the right pieces to decorate your new home.

Who is Hua Hin best suited for? If you're drawn to a quieter beach lifestyle with a strong expat presence, excellent dining options, and a variety of housing options, Hua Hin could be your ideal new home. Just keep in mind that it's a bit farther from Bangkok.

Phetchabun, Nakohn Sawan, and surrounding provinces

If your Thai family is based in the central provinces north of Bangkok—such as Phetchabun and Nakhon Sawan—you'll have the opportunity to enjoy a much more traditional and laid back experience. It takes some reflection and candid conversations with your spouse to settle in these places. Not because they lack beauty (Phetchabun is stunning with its mountains and lush forests), but because living here means many fewer interactions with other expats or Thais who can speak English. Menus in the local restaurants, for instance, are only in Thai.

That said, there are clear advantages. For me personally, being surrounded by a loving and supportive Thai family is priceless. Waking up and enjoying breakfast that comes from the family farm is deeply satisfying and delicious. The cost of living in the provinces is noticeably lower than in more developed parts of Thailand. Pha's visits to the salon are 80 THB and a haircut is 70 THB, where in Bangkok prices start at 400 THB for these services. It's also a great place to live for those who want a contemplative life. When I'm serenaded by songbirds as I write at the farm or do yoga on the front porch, I feel a deep sense of joy. While you'll still have access to popular grocery chains like Makro and Lotus's, finding high-quality medical care can be more challenging, which could be a problem if you have a serious health condition. It's also important to note that economic opportunities for expats are limited in this region, as the local economy is primarily agriculture based. So unless you're working remotely or retired, this may not be the ideal choice.

Who are the central provinces best suited for? If you have a Thai family or love the quiet country life, and don't mind living a Thai lifestyle away from a substantial expat community, the central provinces could be the rural retreat you've been dreaming of. Learning some Thai and really accepting Thai culture is a must.

Northern Thailand

Famous for its regional food, mountainous landscapes, and rich culture, Northern Thailand has plenty to offer expats looking for both developed city life and a proximity to some of the country's most beautiful national forests. The region's most popular expat hub is also one of Thailand's largest cities. Let's start there.

Chiang Mai

Considered the epicenter of Northern Thai culture, Chiang Mai is a bustling city that surrounds the old walled city replete with ancient temples and ruins. Alongside the historic sites is a modern metropolis complete with mega malls, trendy cafes, and large universities.

If you're a nature lover, Chiang Mai offers all the benefits of modern city living combined with easy access to trekking, rafting, and cycling. Beyond its mountainous skyline lies Doi Inthanon, a national park home to Thailand's highest peak, dense forests, and waterfalls. What's more, if you're looking for a break from Thailand's intense heat, Chiang Mai's cooler "winter" mornings often dip into the 50s (mid-teens Celsius), and occasionally you'll see Thais posting pictures of frost on the ground.

There are many things that attract expats to Chiang Mai, including quality hospitals, a US Consulate, and an excellent restaurant scene, featuring both international cuisine and northern Thai specialties like khao soi (my favorite curry) and sai ua, a wonderfully spicy and herbaceous northern Thai sausage. While the city is a major tourist destination with an international airport, its size and diverse neighborhoods make it easy to escape the crowds. Finally, if you're looking to connect with other foreigners, Chiang Mai is also home to a large expat community, offering plenty of opportunities to talk about the news from the home country.

Who is Chiang Mai best suited for? If you're looking for a city lifestyle with close access to nature and outdoor adventures, Chiang Mai could be the perfect place to call home. There are business opportunities, good international schools, and an international airport, making this an attractive alternative to Bangkok for expat families of working age.

Other destinations in Northern Thailand

Beyond Chiang Mai's borders, you'll find cities and towns that are a bit more rural and remote, each offering its own unique character. Here are some of the best options for expats looking for something different.

Chiang Rai

Similar to Chiang Mai but on a smaller scale, Chiang Rai is a nice blend of city convenience and rural charm. While it's not as developed as Chiang Mai, you'll still find Western-style condos and housing developments, popular restaurant chains, and hip cafes. The expat community is smaller and the city has a more laid back feel. In fact, if you journey to its outskirts, you'll quickly feel like you're in the country, with its open landscapes and more rustic houses. There are also tea plantations and a Swiss style chalet and gardens constructed by the Queen Mother of King Rama IX. The annual flower festival is a lovely way to spend an evening or two. Oh, and I'd be remiss if I failed to mention that if you're driving from Chiang Rai to Chiang Mai, a must stop is the Charin Garden Pie Resort. That's right, a resort located in the middle of a forest dedicated to the art of making delicious American pies, handcrafted by a retired Thai nurse who spent much of her career in Chicago. Now, I mention this because, yes, the pies are fantastic, but also because around almost any corner and in every community of the Kingdom there are these little gems to discover. The only problem is too little time and deciding between the key lime, apple crumble, or pumpkin.

What Chiang Rai lacks in urban development, it makes up for with natural beauty, a slower pace of life, and small-town vibe. Like Chiang Mai, it also enjoys cooler winter temperatures, offering a refreshing break from Thailand's tropical heat.

Who is Chiang Rai best suited for? If Chiang Mai feels too urbanized and you're looking for a city with a more relaxed, rural atmosphere, Chiang Rai is a good choice.

KNOW
BEFORE YOU GO

THE REALITY OF NORTHERN THAILAND'S SMOKY SEASON

When considering a move to Northern Thailand, it's important to be aware of the smoky season, which typically lasts sometime between January to April and affects the entire region. This is caused by farmers burning excess vegetation. During this period, air quality can be quite poor. While much of Thailand experiences bad air quality during this time of year, the north tends to experience the worst of it.

That said, the region's natural beauty, relaxed pace of life, and vibrant culture continue to attract expats from around the world. While the smoky season is a factor to consider, many people who move here find ways to manage it, whether by traveling during peak months, using air purifiers, or adapting their routines. If you're drawn to Northern Thailand's charm, I encourage you to consider the locations listed here and see if the region's many rewards outweigh its seasonal challenges.

Nan

Nan is a testament to Thailand's enduring culture and diversity. Located in the northeast corner of the Kingdom, this hidden gem is a throwback to Thailand's pace of life from 75 years ago. Its rolling mountains and verdant forests create a lush landscape worth exploring. In town, its traditional night market offers public places to grab some traditional food, sit on the lawn dotted with woven mats, and eat off of low tables while listening to live music as the sun sets. There are also local crafts shops exhibiting the talents and traditions of the region's silversmiths and textile weavers.

Despite being about an hour flight from Bangkok, fewer foreign tourists make their way here. And life moves at a much slower pace. While you won't find big city attractions and entertainment, Nan does have good housing options and a welcomed low cost of living.

Who is Nan best suited for? If you love a slower pace of life nestled in a valley surrounded by mountains, want to be immersed in Thai culture with fewer expats or foreign tourists, and enjoy a more traditional way of life, Nan is a great place to call home.

Pai

The first time we rolled into Pai, after driving up a mountain through 737 hairpin curves (yes, it's been counted), we tucked into the first decent looking restaurant with a menu boasting macrobiotics and cold pressed juices. I was wondering if I had wandered into an old hippie town in Northern California. And it turns out we had. Tucked away in a mountain valley about a three hour drive from Chiang Mai, Pai is a close knit community that values living in harmony with nature. In other words, it's a great place to break out the tie dyed tee from your last Grateful Dead concert. As expected, you'll find plenty of yoga studios, dreadlocks, and a very cool night market lining almost the length of this laid back town.

Getting to Pai is an adventure in itself, as the winding mountain road from Chiang Mai is replete with motorbikes, gasoline trucks, and locals in a hurry. It's not a drive for the faint of heart. As Pai is quite isolated, expect to tackle that road regularly if you need frequent access to Chiang Mai or its international airport.

Who is Pai best suited for? If you're a free spirit at heart, a nature enthusiast, and looking for a community of like minded individuals, Pai might just be your paradise.

Eastern Thailand

When I refer to the east here, I'm specifically talking about one of Thailand's most overlooked regions: Isaan. It's one of the country's biggest producers of rice and sticky rice, grown mostly on small family farms, and is therefore the least economically developed area of the Kingdom. It offers a truly authentic Thai experience for those willing to venture off the beaten path or who have married into the community. The regional cuisine from Isaan is my favorite in all of Thailand, which is not surprising as most poor rural areas learn to make delicious food with the simplest and freshest ingredients. This is home of som tam (papaya salad) and larb (minced pork or chicken), both of which are typically amped up with a large dose of Thai chilies.

Isaan is also home to several major cities, including Khon Kaen, Udon Thani, and Ubon Ratchathani. However, I've chosen to only focus on Korat (also known as Nakhon Ratchasima), as it is the third largest city in Thailand and arguably the most expat-friendly of Isaan's cities.

Korat

Korat is often referred to as the gateway to Isaan, as it serves as the main entry point to this culturally rich region. Despite being one of the largest cities in the country, Korat has a relatively small expat population. English isn't as widely spoken here. And even if you speak Thai, the Isaan dialect with its unique vocabulary and similarity to Lao will be another challenge to master. In short, living in Korat requires a special kind of expat—someone who's willing to adapt and integrate more deeply into Thai culture.

That said, as a major city, Korat is fairly well developed. You'll find modern and reputable hospitals, large Western-style shopping centers, and plenty of condos for sale or rent. Since Korat isn't a tourist destination, your money will go notably further here with a friendly local population unharried by catering to the tourist trade. With a very low cost of living, especially for a city of its size, this is an attractive option for budget-conscious expats who love delicious, locally raised food.

Another major perk of living in Korat is its proximity to one of Thailand's most famous national parks, Khao Yai, just an hour and a half drive away. Here, you'll find hiking trails, wildlife, waterfalls, and beautiful natural landscapes. However, you don't have to rough it, as there are many lovely resorts for every budget. If you're into the outdoors, it's a must-visit place in Thailand.

Who is Korat best suited for? If you're seeking an authentic Thai experience, a low cost of living, and the adventure of big city living with fewer foreigners and limited English spoken, Korat may be the right choice for you. Also, if you have a Thai spouse from Issan, this may be a good bridge between being close to the family on the farm and having the amenities a large city has to offer.

Southern Thailand

Do you hear that ukulele? Yes, we've arrived at white sand beaches and crystal clear waters, and what often comes to mind when people think of Thailand. The south is truly a paradise for those who look forward to daily sunrise walks by the water and practicing yoga cooled by a sea breeze. Below are three popular southern destinations that many expats choose to call home.

Phuket

One of the most famous places in Thailand (and arguably one of the world's top beach destinations) is Phuket. Like Pattaya, Phuket attracts a large number of tourists and boasts a sizable expat community from around the world. So why choose Phuket over Pattaya? Phuket offers more natural beauty, opportunities for diving, and has some of the most developed infrastructure in the south, including private hospitals and acclaimed international schools. While the water is clear and beautiful and limestone cliffs dot the landscape, with all that development and tourism comes heavy traffic at rush hour and high season, and less tranquil environments than you'll find on less populated isles. That's the tradeoff with Phuket. Also on the plus side, it is a convenient jumping-off point for exploring the rest of the south, with relatively easy access to Koh Phi Phi and Koh Lanta, and an international airport with many daily domestic and international flight options.

As is true with many beach and island enclaves globally, Phuket is decidedly more expensive than many other places in Thailand, including Pattaya. Despite the availability of condos, apartments, and luxury villas, demand for rentals and real estate is high. Now, you can eat and play more affordably than the average tourist by going to local markets, and with snorkel and mask in hand, almost all beach access is free of charge.

Who is Phuket best suited for? If you want upscale beach living, value natural beauty, and don't mind a higher cost of living—or sharing paradise with plenty of other foreigners—Phuket might be your perfect new home. It may also suit the liveaboard sailors, thanks to well equipped marinas, as well as families who are looking for great schools and a beach lifestyle.

Samui

If you're looking to live the picture book island life, Koh Samui may be the best option on this list. While Phuket is technically an island, it doesn't always feel like one because of its size, busy roads, and high season crowds. Samui on the other hand offers much quieter areas outside of the tourist heavy zones around the airport and Chaweng beach. This tropical island in the Gulf of Thailand is the closest thing to the Hawaiian island of Kauai, offering comfort and amenities as well as seclusion and peace. And even if you choose a remote jungle hideaway, the ocean is rarely more than a quick motorbike drive away.

As a popular destination, Samui naturally draws a lot of tourists, especially after a certain popular TV series highlighted its beauty. Still, it's also home to a large expat community, offering a sense of connection for foreigners living abroad.

If you like island hopping, Koh Samui is close to other famous islands known for diving and snorkeling (including Koh Tao and Koh Pha Ngan). It's also near the stunning Mu Ko Ang Thong National Marine Park—known for its inspiring limestone islands and kayaking. A bonus is Koh Samui has its own airport, with direct flights to Bangkok in a little over an hour.

If you're drawn to the ocean and dream of living the true island life, Samui offers an idyllic setting. Just keep in mind that, as one of Thailand's most popular islands, it comes with a higher cost of living.

Who is Samui best suited for? If you're an ocean lover seeking a laid-back island lifestyle and don't mind some isolation from mainland Thailand—or the higher prices—Samui is a wonderful place to call home.

Krabi

Don't let the fact that Krabi is the only non-island in this last section deter you from considering this otherwise genuine beach destination. Krabi boasts some of the most awesome, raw natural beauty in all of Thailand. From the limestone karsts jutting out of its emerald-green waters to the mangrove forests and cascading waterfalls dotted across its lush landscape, Krabi is ideal for nature lovers.

If you love the outdoors and the beach, Krabi offers endless opportunities for adventure. You can scuba dive, snorkel, kayak, and rock climb on its dramatic cliffs, all while exploring the province's many islands.

From a purely day-to-day living perspective, Krabi sees fewer tourists than Koh Samui and Phuket, making it easier to escape popular beach spots to find peaceful, secluded areas. With its laid back vibe and pristine surroundings, many parts of Krabi feel like your own private paradise.

Who is Krabi best suited for? If you're an outdoors and beach lover who prefers fewer tourists and expats, and wishes to enjoy some of Thailand's most stunning natural scenery, Krabi may just be the little slice of paradise you've been searching for. International travel will require more time and planning, but there is an airport with daily flights to Bangkok.

EXPAT PERSPECTIVE #4

Long time legal powerhouse

IRA E. BLUMENTHAL
PARTNER | BLUMENTHAL RICHTER & SUMET

www.brslawyers.com

What is your background, and what brought you to Thailand?

I grew up in Brooklyn, New York, during the 70-80s, which was a pretty tough time to be in the city. I attended City College and then Georgetown Law.

My brother was working in Thailand in the late 1980s. My first year of law school was very tough and I remember sitting in the law school library during a cold February in 1991. I decided that I wanted to do something fun and different during my 1L summer. I then faxed resumes to a few firms in Bangkok. I was offered an internship at a big Thai law firm working for an expat lawyer from Connecticut. It was a fascinating summer. The partner allowed me to join meetings where recognizable multi-national companies were deciding to invest in Thailand. The energy and excitement around all the incoming foreign investment hooked me.

EXPAT PERSPECTIVE

I also loved the energy of Bangkok. It was like New York, but in a foreign country. A 24 hour a day city, where there was always a new experience to be had and something to surprise you. I also loved the dichotomy between old and new. Skyscrapers and spirit houses. Mercedes and elephants on Sukhumvit Road. Bangkok had such a unique energy, which it still retains to this day.

What was the biggest surprise or something you didn't expect when you relocated here?

The biggest surprise for me was how welcoming both the Thai and expat community were towards newcomers. Being a New Yorker, I was definitely not accustomed to people being genuinely open to new people and friendships. Of course, I heard the reputation of Thai people being hospitable, but it was something I had never experienced being raised in NY and studying in DC.

I was also taken aback by how welcoming the expat community was towards a new, young and broke foreigner just starting his career. I became quick friends with everyone from other young expats to Embassy staff to Country Managing Directors. The expat community was a small dynamic village.

What is a bit of wisdom you wish someone had shared with you as you were making Thailand home?

Invest in personal and professional relationships, and take even more business risks, provided they are calculated and well thought out risks.

EXPAT PERSPECTIVE

One of the most rewarding parts of making Thailand my home was the personal and professional relationships I made over thirty years. I have met a lot of really great and dynamic Thais and expats. I also think the unique Thai culture has impacted me in a very positive way and has helped me grow as a person. I have become more accepting, forgiving, patient and more at peace with myself.

Professionally I wish I had taken even more risks in the 90s when the market was really just opening up. I started my firm in 1997. I invested in various businesses, with differing degrees of success, over 30 years. Fortunately, I have been very lucky in my time here and I would encourage expats to take smart, calculated business risks when they see an exciting opportunity. However they should exercise the same good business judgement they would use in their home countries.

Chapter 5:
HOW

*How to navigate Thai culture,
stay safe, and thrive in your new home*

You've chosen where you want to live, at least for a while, and you're excited to explore, make friends, and build a life in your new home. But as your days in Thailand turn into weeks, you start noticing things don't quite work the way they did in your home country. The assumptions you make just don't square with how certain things are turning out. It can feel a bit disorienting. It's like moving into a new house and searching for the light switch in the middle of the night. Everything just feels a little off. Maybe it's how punctuality isn't a major concern or the way smiles can mean a dozen different things. A number of social norms you've lived by your entire life have suddenly gone out the window, like saying "Bless you" when someone sneezes or patting a child affectionately on the head. When you interact with locals, it's hard to tell whether you're truly being understood, something that will become apparent at restaurants when surprising dishes show up at the table. How do you best adapt to this strange yet exciting new world?

Don't worry, time and experience will be your best guide. In this chapter, I'll cover what I've learned, sometimes the hard way, about Thai social norms and how to productively interact with locals while avoiding faux pas. In other words, we're diving into Thai culture. Understanding these nuances will save you from unnecessary frustration and help you build positive relationships with Thai family, friends, co-workers and staff, and folks you interact with every day.

We'll also explore common annoyances Westerners encounter, along with how to stay safe and comfortable in your new home. So, ready to get started? Let's begin with some fundamentals so you better enjoy your time in the Kingdom.

Thai culture 101 (A layman's perspective)

In Chapter 2, I mentioned how Thais will reflect your mood and intentions; happiness will be greeted with a smile, and impatience will produce a less than ideal outcome. This concept is a fundamental part of Thai culture and influences your everyday interactions, which is why it's important to address it first. Thai culture is highly sensitive to the energy you project—when you put out positive energy, you'll receive it in return. Show respect and wai, and you'll be met with the same courtesy. Make an attempt to communicate in Thai, and you'll be praised effusively for your efforts. On the other hand, if you become angry and, as my wife says, "show your face," expect the person you're dealing with to shut down.

As you can probably tell, becoming self-aware of the energy you project is really important in Thailand. For me, it presented a valuable growth opportunity and helped me to become more conscious of how my actions and emotions impact those around me. It's a bit humbling, and as the Buddha teaches, I am mere eons of lifetimes away from enlightenment.

Out of all the traits you could cultivate, the Buddhist ideal of patience is perhaps the most important. After being here a few months, you'll likely hear the phrase "Thai time." This term refers to the Thais relaxed approach to punctuality. Being late for gatherings, meetings, or even home renovations taking longer than expected is quite common in Thailand. In fact, delays are generally not seen as a big deal. Life moves at its own pace here.

It's important to understand that Thai time isn't about being lazy or inefficient. Instead, it reflects Thailand's cultural emphasis on living in the moment and enjoying life. It also reflects the reality of getting around major metropolitan areas where traffic, flooding during the rainy season, or unexpected road closures can mean showing up two or three hours after the appointed time to meet. While adjusting to this mindset can take some getting used to, if you approach it with a sense of humor and patience, your experience will be much more enjoyable. And besides, some unexpected free time presents the opportunity to find a snack or iced coffee at the local market while you're waiting.

Another cultural trait to be aware of is the non-confrontational nature of Thais, which you may have already picked up on from the fact that few locals honk their horns. It's worth exploring this characteristic in more detail, as it's quite different from Western culture.

Consider a common situation you're likely to encounter at some point in Thailand. You're at a restaurant, and the waiter brings you the wrong dish. Instead of getting pad thai, you are served pad see ew. If you were in your home country, what would you do? You'd simply tell the staff, and they'd correct the order. No problem at all. In Thailand, most locals would handle the situation entirely differently. Rather than asking for the correct order, they'd likely eat what was served. Why is this?

It's helpful to understand the Thai concept of kreng jai. This term means to have a deep consideration for others' feelings and to avoid inconveniencing them. Simply put, Thai people prefer not to cause others to lose face or be embarrassed, choosing instead to keep interactions light and harmonious while avoiding confrontation whenever possible.

With this in mind, direct communication can be challenging in Thailand. My advice? Go with the flow and avoid making a fuss unless it's absolutely necessary. But when those situations do arise, the key is to be direct in the most gentle and polite way possible. And always with a smile, of course.

For instance, if a neighbor is playing music too loudly, check any hint of anger or frustration and making a demand. Instead, walk over calmly, knock on the door, and kindly ask with a smile to lower the volume. In most cases, Thais will be happy to oblige as long as your request is delivered with genuine politeness and respect.

Along with the concepts of non-confrontation and kreng jai, Thai culture emphasizes the group over the individual. I believe this starts with prioritizing family needs over individual desires. In fact, after a few months of living in the Kingdom, you'll discover that Thais love doing things together and don't place as much importance on personal space as Westerners do. While we may value our privacy and alone time, Thais prefer shared experiences. It's rare to see a Thai person eating alone or even spending time in solitude.

Group minivan trips are a favorite pastime for Thais. During these events, close to a dozen friends or family members will cram into a van and spend the day together, enjoying all kinds of activities and meals together. These full day excursions might take some getting used to, but if you adopt the mindset of being the leaf in the stream, you'll soon find them second nature. Who knows, you may even grow to like them.

Should you learn Thai?

If you move to a big city like Bangkok or Chiang Mai, you may be hesitant to learn Thai. Why? The truth is, it's not really necessary in these major cities. Many Thais speak sufficient English for you to get by, or you're spending significant time hanging out with other expats. That said, I recommend learning the language, regardless of where you live in the Kingdom. Here's why.

- **You'll get more out of your experience:** If you can speak at an intermediate conversational level in any country, you're bound to have greater and more satisfying interactions with your neighbors, local vendors, service providers, and government officials. Being able to read the language means understanding street signs and, more importantly for me, menus. If learning a new culture is like peeling the layers of an onion, speaking Thai will allow you to go deeper more quickly.

- **Locals appreciate it:** As mentioned in Chapter 2, the locals greatly appreciate you speaking their language. Even if you can only hold a basic conversation about food or where you're from, they'll smile and shower you with compliments on your language skills ("phud Thai geng"). I think simply exhibiting the effort to learn shows appreciation and respect for an ancient language only spoken here. Personally, the joy I feel from these interactions is enough to motivate my learning, and I imagine you may feel the same once you've experienced it yourself.

- **Reading helps with pronunciation:** Thai is a phonetic language to an extent. This means that words are generally pronounced as they are written in Thai, though the English transliteration can be misleading. In other words, learning to read Thai will significantly improve your pronunciation and help you avoid common mistakes made by foreigners. For example, many foreigners pronounce Koh Samui by using a hard "K" sound for "Koh." In reality, the correct pronunciation uses a "G" sound, and the "oh" is pronounced "aw." So instead of "Koh," the correct pronunciation is "Gaw." Being able to read Thai allows you to pick up on these nuances, making communication with locals easier, even as you're still contending with the five tones—high, low, middle, rising, and falling. Reading also allows you to see these tone markers, and listening to Thai (on an app or with family) will help you learn to "sing" the language like a Thai. Again, you will get credit for trying, and the more you take that leap the better you'll get. If you have the courage to try one day, you'll have those satisfying moments of interacting effectively in Thai in a variety of circumstances.

Respect is at the heart of Thai culture

By now, you can probably tell that respect plays a significant role in Thai culture. Showing respect not only helps you avoid unintentionally offending locals. It can also lead to better service at restaurants, banks, and immigration offices, as the people and culture will be more receptive to you. However, respect in Thailand is multifaceted and can be expressed in a variety of ways. Let's talk about them.

Shoes: In Thai and Buddhist culture, feet are considered the lowest part of the body—both physically and symbolically—since they are furthest from the most sacred part, the head. As such, you'll often see Thais remove their shoes in many public places, like temples and some shops, to show respect and maintain cleanliness. What's more, you'll never see them wearing shoes inside their home or when visiting friends. Point being, if you see a bunch of shoes outside a building, be sure to take yours off before entering.

Clothing: Perhaps one of the most painful contradictions of Thailand is that it can be ungodly hot, yet you're often expected to skip the shorts and flip flops and don long pants and closed toe shoes. Why is this? While this may sound unusual, in Thailand, covering extremities is seen as a sign of maturity and showing respect to others. After all, here it's the kids who wear shorts to school, while mom and dad dress appropriately for work. As mentioned earlier, shorts are definitely inappropriate for government offices, and this also extends to business settings, official events, and temple visits. In all of these situations, it's the norm and a sign of proper etiquette to wear pants, shirts that cover the shoulders, and skirts that cover the knees.

Temples: While temples were mentioned in the previous points, there's a little more you should know about them. In addition to removing your shoes, wearing pants, and covering your shoulders, it's important to be respectful at temples as they hold deep cultural and spiritual significance for Thais. That means take off your hat and speak quietly. Kneeling or sitting on the prayer rugs in front of the Buddha is expected, and your feet should never be pointed toward the Buddha or a monk. Monks are also forbidden from making physical contact with women, so handing something to a monk directly should be avoided. All of this said, please don't worry, as monks practice universal compassion and patience. You will be welcomed at temples if you practice mindfulness and do your best to be respectful. You will also have the opportunity to leave a small donation in the many cash boxes you'll see in the sanctuaries, but this is not required. Give as you see fit.

Horn honking: I've touched on this a few times already, so I won't discuss it much here. However, it's worth noting that horn honking is perceived very differently in Thailand compared to places like New York, India, or Vietnam, where it can be seen as a form of communication. In Thailand, honking can be viewed as a sign of disrespect, impatience, and anger. It is also likely to trigger passive aggressive responses from Thai drivers, such as slowing down, blocking your path, or braking unexpectedly. Use your horn sparingly and only when absolutely necessary when safety requires.

The Royal Family: The Thai Royal Family is deeply revered and expected to be treated with the utmost respect. This deference is so ingrained in Thai culture that before every movie screening, the royal anthem is played alongside a video montage of the Royal Family, during which everyone in the theater (including you) is expected to stand. Never, under any circumstances, make negative comments about the Royal Family in public. Doing so could result in severe consequences, including legal sanctions, as Thailand has a strict lèse majesté law that criminalizes such remarks. Unlike in some Western countries, freedom of speech is not an absolute right in Thailand, so you must mind your words carefully when it comes to the monarchy. You have, after all, relocated to the Kingdom of Thailand.

Government and businesses: Just as with the Royal Family, it's important to be cautious when commenting on businesses and the government in Thailand. While lawsuits are uncommon, a scathing review of a hotel or business could lead to legal action, as Thai business owners may view it as defamation. This is especially true if someone makes repeated comments to harm a business in retaliation for perceived bad service. Publicly criticizing the government could have similar consequences and even potential loss of legal status and expulsion from the country. When in doubt, it's best to approach such topics with diplomacy and discretion. And with all interactions here, check your anger, as the Buddha teaches anger is the manifestation of intent to do harm.

Age and position: In Thailand, age and social position are viewed quite differently than in the West. Older individuals are revered, or at least respected, and often given preference in social and professional settings. Titles also carry significant weight. The more important a person's title, the more respect they're shown. You'll quickly notice that the Thai language reflects this cultural emphasis on hierarchy. For instance, older individuals are commonly addressed as "Pee," while younger folks are called "Nong." There are also different Thai words for older and younger relatives within the family. When in doubt, you can always show respect by addressing someone as Kuhn (sir or madam) and putting a "K." in front of their name when sending an email.

Don't sweat the small stuff

The timeless saying "Don't sweat the small stuff" has a couple of Thai variations commonly spoken here: Mai pen rai (no big deal) and alai godai (whatever). The truth is, if you want to feel more content in Thailand, it's helpful to accept local customs that may occasionally test your patience. Remember, even though this new culture can present challenges to the way you're used to seeing things back home, it's really mai pen rai.

A common frustration among expats you'll see on social media is dual pricing. If you visit a national park or historical site, you'll likely be charged significantly higher than Thais, sometimes up to ten times as much. Now, putting this in context we're talking about 300 THB versus 30 THB ($9 versus a dollar). If this upsets you, try to keep things in perspective. While you might have to pay a higher price at some attractions, after your visit you can still enjoy a delicious local meal for just a few dollars. In the grand scheme of things, Thailand's low cost of living far outweighs the occasional differential charge. Now, as you settle in here, you can also apply for a pink Thai ID card (Thai nationals have a blue card). I show this at these attractions and say, "Pom ben kon Thai," which means "I'm Thai" in English. Hey, about half the time it works and I pay the locals' rate, and as a bonus I get to amuse the ticket taker.

The same advice applies to 90-day residential reporting. You might feel that, after living in Thailand for years and being a contributor to the Kingdom, you shouldn't have to report where you reside every 90 days. The reality is, things work differently here, and there's little point in fighting the system. Just like dual pricing, there are some things you'll just have to accept (alai godai). Whether it's dogs barking in the middle of the night, people driving on the wrong side of the road, loud music from a nearby festival blaring into your condo, or groups of people blocking your pathway on an already overcrowded sidewalk, some aspects of Thai culture are beyond our control.

Ultimately, you've moved to a place where space and time have different meanings, so be kind to yourself and patient with the locals. There will be moments of frustration where you find yourself thinking, "Are you kidding me?!," but we can all learn from our challenges. As the old saying goes, accept the things you cannot change,[7] summon the courage to change the things you can, and have the wisdom to know the difference. Or, in Buddhist parlance, "If it weren't for these moments of frustration, what would teach me patience?"

Even if you still find yourself getting frustrated by local customs, give yourself some credit, as you may be surprised by how much progress you've made when you next visit your home country. Let me share a couple stories to illustrate this. A few years ago, my wife and I visited family in the UK and were waiting for a train to take us from Maidstone back to London, which was running three minutes late. While we hardly thought this was in any way a delay, once we boarded I was surprised to hear the conductor apologizing to passengers and giving a lengthy explanation over the minor holdup. Not only wasn't I bothered, but I was grateful the train arrived at all.

This goes to show how Thailand can have a positive effect on you, helping you recognize the patience and adaptability you've mastered when you're suddenly back "in Kansas." You might be surprised at how

---

[7] Accept the things you cannot change. Niebuhr, Reinhold. "The Serenity Prayer." 1934.

much you've changed when a small delay that once frustrated you now barely registers.

A similar situation happened on another visit back when I was picking up a to-go order with a good friend at a Thai restaurant in Los Angeles. Our food was an hour late, as the Thai kitchen staff was just overwhelmed with orders. While my friend was visibly stressed about the wait, I felt completely at ease. I'm not saying this to brag—I still have plenty to learn from Thailand, and my patience is tested regularly. But living here long enough fundamentally changes your perceptions about expecting perfection and accepting circumstances as they arise. So, do your best not to sweat the small stuff in Thailand. You'll enjoy life here a lot more if you do.

Family and land hold different meanings in Thailand

Now that we've covered some of the basics of Thai culture, let's dive into two aspects of it that are deeply ingrained in Thai society: family and land. These values are so central to life in Thailand that they deserve their own dedicated discussion. Let's talk about family first.

Family

In Thailand, the way family is thought of here will appear far different than it is in the West. In some respects, I'd go as far to say that it's a 180 degree change in perception. While in the West, parents are focused on taking care of their kids and doing everything to make them happy, in Thailand children are expected to treat their parents with that same level of devotion—taking care of them and prioritizing their happiness. In the

West, children are encouraged to speak their minds and let their parents know what they want or need ("use your words"). In Thailand, children are taught to never speak back to their parents and take what they're told as gospel.

This cultural philosophy is especially important to keep in mind if you plan to marry a Thai. Marriage in Thailand isn't just about joining lives with one person. You're essentially marrying into their family as well. This can have significant implications for your relationship, particularly if you're not fully prepared for the cultural expectations that come with this commitment.

If you're marrying a Thai partner, be aware that their parents may have significant influence over important aspects of your spouse's life, including where you live, your spouse's job, and financial contributions to the family from both you and your partner. Let me share a real life example. My Thai teacher lives in Phuket, nearly 300 miles away from her parents in Hat Yai. Yet, whenever they ask her to return home, she does so at the drop of a hat. She simply gets in the car, drives seven hours, and takes care of whatever they need. In Thailand, parents are held in the highest regard, and many adult children will do whatever they ask without question or voicing complaints or concerns.

This is why it's vital to have an open conversation with your partner about family expectations before getting married. Especially since foreign spouses are sometimes viewed as a source of support by Thai parents, just like they view their sons and daughters. Also, there is an assumption that all expats are wealthy, at least relatively so, and there's a corresponding expectation that the wealth can be shared. That said, not all Thai families think this way. With my Thai family, I feel as though I've received much more than I've contributed in terms of love, support, and inclusion. And while I've been happy to provide what's needed, they've never asked me for anything. Again, this is a conversation you should have with your partner before tying the knot, which is probably a good idea in any context, but certainly in Thailand.

The last thing to mention here while we're on the topic of Thai relationships is their tradition of dowries, which are still common in Thailand (although my spouse had less than no interest in this ritual). If you're unfamiliar with the term, it refers to a sum of money the groom pays to the bride's family upon marriage. You may be expected to offer one, sometimes making a show of it at the ceremony in gold or cash. Again, it isn't always expected, and it may be returned in full in the form of a gift like a car or house. Either way, it's important to discuss this topic with your partner in advance of your wedding to avoid surprises.

Land

Another fundamental part of Thai culture is land and the intrinsic value it holds. Thais perceive land much differently than Westerners. Most Western cultures view land as a commodity or investment, and even the family home can be viewed as a way to accumulate wealth. Not so for most Thais.

For example, when Pha and I were looking to purchase a rice farm (nah cao) in Phetchabun, I asked her family about what kind of return on investment we could get from a typical harvest or how much we could receive in income if we rented the land to a farmer. In my mind, I'm judging the land purchase by comparing the return I was getting from my investment accounts to what income the land could yield from the sale of a harvest less expenses. Spoiler alert, rice farming in Thailand is not highly lucrative. However, my Thai family didn't see the property as an investment. To them, it was a beautiful piece of land near Meh Joop's house and would establish the family as more substantial land holders in their community, with the attendant status that goes with that ownership. Besides, my family holds the view that land always goes up in value.

The family farm in Nong Phai, Phetchabun

So for many Thais, particularly in farm communities in the provinces, land isn't primarily viewed as a financial investment but rather as a source of autonomy, status, and pride. The land is in essence their kingdom, their domain. It's likely the reason that when I speak with many locals, their dream is to retire to a nice piece of farm land they own. To reside in a peaceful setting over which they exert complete dominion and control is the ideal for spending their golden years. For many of my relatives in the US, the dream was cashing out of the family home, leaving the snow shovel in the garage, and retiring to a golf community in an easy to care for condo in Florida or Arizona.

This value placed in land ownership is so ingrained in Thai culture that the two most meaningful documents to Thais are their ID number (like a US social security number) and their Tabian Baan, which is their house registration. This cultural significance is also partially why foreigners can only purchase land in Thailand by becoming Thai citizens. Land is seen as something of intrinsic value. Ownership is reserved for those who were born here or have demonstrated a long term and deep enough commitment to the Kingdom to be granted the privilege of citizenship.

Safety, comfort, and keeping your peace of mind

Thailand is a developing country. And while Bangkok is a world class city with sophisticated infrastructure, out in the provinces (where we live much of the time) it's a different story. So, if you're like many Westerners, you probably have questions about how safe it is and the level of comfort you can expect. Do you have to worry about things like robbery? Is food poisoning common? How intense is the heat, and does it flood during the rainy season? Let's explore these concerns, starting with a topic that has brought Thailand into the headlines in recent years.

Roads and finding religion

Most newcomers to the Land of Smiles probably don't realize it, but Thailand has consistently ranked among the countries with the most dangerous roads in the world. Most recently, the World Health

Organization ranked it 16th for most traffic fatalities worldwide.[8] If you ever hop on a motorbike taxi, you'll quickly understand why. The roads can seem chaotic. Cars are jam packed into narrow lanes, spilling over onto the shoulder as motorcycles weave between vehicles or simply travel the wrong direction on the highway's shoulder. I've learned to always look both directions before making a turn or entering a highway, just in case a motorbike is coming illegally from the left. There are a number of unwritten rules of the road here and, like most lessons in life, experience will be your best guide.

Also, your risk tolerance may be different than mine. The first time I rode on the back of a motorbike taxi, I found religion. With each bob and weave through traffic, seeming inches away from the vehicles we were blithely passing, I was praying under my breath, "Oh my god, oh my god." Then I saw a 20-something Thai office lady in heels and a skirt riding side saddle on another motorbike taxi in the next lane, completely engrossed in her phone as if she were lounging in a café. Talk about feeling like a wimp. At that point I relaxed a bit, at least until the next near miss of the car alongside us.

The unpredictability of u-turns

While u-turns are a common feature on roads worldwide, in Thailand they can be particularly hazardous as many are located on highways. So, if you're cruising along on a four lane highway at 120 kilometers per hour and see a u-turn ahead, stay alert. A truck or car may attempt a u-

---

8 The World Health Organization ranked it 16th. "Road traffic death rate (per 100 000 population), estimate," World Health Organization, accessed July 8, 2025. https://www.who.int/data/gho/data/indicators/indicator-details/GHO/estimated-road-traffic-death-rate-(per-100-000-population)

turn—even if it's not the most opportune time. Flashing your lights at a vehicle that may appear to be unsafely turning in front of you is acceptable and prudent. Simply put, defensive driving is important on Thai roads. If you ever get in an accident, you'll be expected to stay put (even if it's a minor fender bender and you're blocking traffic) until the insurance company and police arrive to document the incident.

Motorbikes and mishaps

While it's easy to be swept up in the joy and adventure of renting a motorbike to cruise around one of Thailand's gorgeous tropical islands, or buying one to get around town, a simple spill can turn into a hospital stay. Motorbike accidents are a major problem in the Land of Smiles. In fact, 74% of Thailand's traffic fatalities involve motorcyclists.[9]

Be mindful that not all insurance providers cover motorbike accidents, and some only cover 50% of medical expenses. If you plan to drive a motorbike in Thailand, get a license. Without one, it's less likely your provider will cover you in the event of an accident. And of course, get a safety tested helmet to protect your most important asset.

---

[9] 74% of Thailand's traffic fatalities. Nichamon Thongphat, Jitlaykha Sukruay, Nichcha Angsuphanich, Pawika Klaharn, "Motorbike death toll, a growing crisis," Bangkok Post, March 15, 2023. https://www.bangkokpost.com/opinion/opinion/2528069/motorbike-death-toll-a-growing-crisis.

Sunburn or soaked?
The tale of Thailand's rainy and hot seasons

Thailand's rainy and hot seasons bring extreme weather that can take some getting used to. The heat and sun can be intense year-round, so it's wise to remain mindful of heat-related risks like heatstroke. Using a bit of common sense like drinking plenty of water, wearing sunscreen, and seeking shade whenever possible will become second nature once you're here for a summer (roo doo rawn, or literally hot season).

During the hot season, this advice becomes even more paramount as temperatures can soar into the 40s centigrade (100+ fahrenheit). The first time I visited Pha's family during Thai summer (March–May), I jumped out of the air conditioned truck and had only walked about 20 feet to the house when I felt decidedly light-headed. A chair was brought out along with two fans, and I sat a while in the shade composing myself. Of course, for years after that, every time I arrived at Meh Joop's house, a chair and two fans were waiting for me. Oh, those dainty farangs.

The rainy season, on the other hand, is marked by sudden downpours and occasional flooding that can make getting around town challenging. Though heavy rains typically last only around an hour, they wreak havoc on traffic and can be a mess if you get stuck outside in one, especially if you forgot your umbrella…not that that's ever happened to me.

So don't be shy about changing plans if you see a downpour coming. Once on a trek down Wireless Road where our offices are located, the street was flooded outside the Vietnam Embassy and I had to remove my shoes, roll up my pants, and wade through about two feet of water to get home. Another day I missed a client appointment when the taxi I was in drove 300 meters, stopped, and turned around having been informed by a fellow driver that the road we were on was impassable.

These occurrences are relatively infrequent, but everyone understands cancellations or late arrivals during the rainy season.

Surviving soi dogs

Adjusting to life in a new country often sheds light on the things you take for granted, and walking, jogging, or cycling in Thailand is no exception. Stray dogs, known as soi dogs, roam neighborhoods freely. While many are quite docile and actually pets owned by locals to protect their properties, you're bound to come across aggressive ones sooner or later. I've had visiting friends return quickly from morning runs after being confronted by loudly barking dogs on our street.

Soi dogs move both alone and in packs, and the aggressive ones won't hesitate to chase you, regardless of whether you're walking, jogging, or even riding a motorbike. If confronted, the key is to remain calm. In my experience, keeping composed and putting out calm energy usually results in the dog sniffing me briefly before walking away.

What doesn't kill you makes you itch

You may remember from Chapter 1 my love of gardening. Well, when we first built our house in Phetchabun, I'd often come back from tending to my plants with unpleasant surprises. "What was this?" I wondered, as I stared in disbelief at the weird bites and rashes on my hands.

After living in Thailand for a while, I became aware of the incredible variety of insects here and have had more than a few run-ins with my least favorite, the red fire ants. So if you're like me and enjoy gardening, wear gloves. Closed toed shoes aren't a bad idea either, and as ever, be mindful before you put your hand in the dirt.

Avoid violent crime with common sense and a smile

Thailand is an incredibly safe country. While violent crime is rare, incidents like bar fights or altercations with taxi drivers do happen. The great news is you can avoid many of these situations with a little bit of common sense. Avoid stumbling drunk down dark alleyways or starting arguments when out late at night. If you ever do find yourself in a confrontation, de-escalate it with a wai, smile, and apology. If you're overcharged following a taxi or tuk tuk ride, my advice is pay the fare. You can report your driver to the traffic or tourist police later. Remember, put out good energy and project the behavior you'd like to receive, and you should be just fine.

Theft without the physical threat

While violent crime is rare, theft is more common in Thailand. That said, it's not the type where you're held up at gunpoint. As mentioned, Thais are non-confrontational by nature, so usually it's quite sneaky, done late at night, or when a house or an apartment is empty. To put this in context, I've been in cities in South America where talking outside on a cell phone is very likely to result in that phone being snatched away. Here, almost everyone is on their cell phones while walking the streets of Bangkok, illustrating just how safe everyone feels about displaying an expensive device in public. My general rule of thumb, in any event, is the less flashy the jewelry the better, and do maintain some sense of situational awareness when you're carrying valuables.

It's worth noting that a lot of theft is drug addiction related or done out of economic need, as there's a big income disparity in Thailand. To protect yourself, lock your doors when leaving home and avoid leaving valuables in plain sight and unattended. If you're building a home, a conspicuously displayed camera system is a good deterrent to would-be thieves looking for an easy mark.

Why health insurance is a must,even when the cost of care is cheap

While medical treatment in Thailand costs a fraction of what it does in the US, or for private care in other Western countries, I still highly recommend getting health insurance. A serious car or motorbike accident or an extended hospital stay could cost you over $100,000. Which is why it's wise to protect yourself against worst case scenarios.

In Thailand, health insurance providers offer two main types of coverage: inpatient and outpatient:

- **Inpatient (IPD):** Covers medical treatments that require an overnight hospital stay and surgical procedures, including most minor ones.

- **Outpatient (OPD):** Covers doctor visits for less serious issues, such as colds, stomach flu, or minor injuries like dog bites.

Everyone should have an inpatient policy, as it provides essential protection. Outpatient coverage is best for those seeking more comprehensive insurance.

While covering the ins and outs of the Thai health insurance system is beyond the scope of this book, I recommend reading this Guide to Expat Health Insurance in Thailand.[10] This guide digs into the intricacies and idiosyncrasies of the system that could have a major impact on your health, including how Thailand handles pre-existing conditions and lifetime renewal guarantees. I also recommend a good broker such as the founder at Seek-to-Insure, Darren, who will know the market and tailor policies to your needs and budget.

Getting the Thai price on taxis and tuk tuks

If you've researched Thailand online, you've likely come across the country's iconic tuk tuks. These small, brightly colored, three-wheeled vehicles offer a fun way to get around. Many long-term expats even have their go-to tuk tuk drivers they use regularly. If it's your first time riding in a tuk tuk, be sure to negotiate the fare upfront. If the price seems too high, don't hesitate to move on to another driver. I would not recommend these vehicles for longer or highway trips, as the lack of doors and seatbelts present some obvious safety risks.

Taxis are another common transportation option. While they are supposed to use the meter, drivers near popular tourist areas like the

---

[10] Guide to Expat Health Insurance. Mark Friedman, "The 2025 Guide to Expat Health Insurance in Thailand: How It Works, Requirements, and Where to Buy," Baan Thai Immigrations Solutions, January 2, 2024. https://btisolutions.co/expat-health-insurance-thailand/

Grand Palace or Asiatique may try to offer a fixed fee instead. If you're unhappy with their quote, you can often find a meter-using driver by walking five minutes away from the tourist hotspot, or you could try the Grab app (Thailand's version of Uber). Indeed, I'd recommend downloading the Grab app for easy access to all forms of transportation—from cars to vans to motorbikes—and for that late night food craving.

Whether you're taking a taxi or a tuk tuk, you'll tend to get a better price and fairer treatment if you request the service in Thai. Know that most taxi drivers do not speak English fluently, so it's a good idea to have your destination written out in Thai. At bottom, Thailand offers plenty of reasonably priced transportation options, including buses, mini-vans, and trains.

Street food and Ice are safer than you think

If you're new to Thailand, you might be concerned about food poisoning or drinking water with ice. Speaking from experience, my friends and I rarely have issues. If you're a bit cautious but still want to try street food, a good rule of thumb is to choose vendors with a line or a steady crowd. A high turnover usually indicates a returning customer base and safe food practices.

All that said, it's important to know that as Thailand is a developing country, cleanliness standards can vary. For example, in Western grocery stores, meat is typically vacuum-sealed and stored on ice, whereas in local markets, it's often displayed unrefrigerated out in the open. Despite these differences, don't assume that food from street vendors or local markets is unsafe. My wife, friends, and I regularly enjoy street food and occasionally shop at local markets with little to no issues. Food is generally safe in Thailand. Just use your best judgment and enjoy the culinary adventure. Finally, bottled water is ubiquitous and can be purchased for as little as 7-10 THB at convenience stores. So safely and cheaply staying hydrated in the Kingdom is easy.

Phone, wallet, keys...and toilet paper?

When heading out for a few hours or longer, it's wise to carry some toilet paper with you. Public bathrooms in Thailand can be hit or miss—sometimes they have toilet paper, sometimes they don't. Upscale restaurants and major Western-style malls typically provide it, but smaller establishments and roadside facilities often don't.

If you're taking a road trip, the ubiquitous PTT gas stations along the highways have the cleanest bathrooms. Again, it's always a good idea to bring your own toilet paper, just in case. If you're a person who runs through the mental checklist of "phone, wallet, keys" when leaving your house, you may want to update it in Thailand to "phone, wallet, keys, toilet paper."

Jail, lawsuits, and treading the legal system carefully

Lawsuits are far less common in Thailand compared to countries like the US and UK, but if you wish to take legal action, it is possible. However, Thai courts generally prefer mediation and settlement over lengthy disputes. If you're expecting a quick resolution by a jury of your peers, know that Thailand doesn't have a jury system, and cases can take a good while to resolve unless you're willing to compromise.

That said, if you do decide to pursue a lawsuit, follow the same precautions outlined in Chapter 3 for hiring contractors and service providers: never pay the full amount upfront and thoroughly vet your lawyer instead of choosing the first firm you find online. In short, protect yourself by doing your due diligence.

When it comes to the criminal justice system, it's something you definitely don't want to experience firsthand. Thai jails are overcrowded with notoriously poor sanitary conditions. To avoid finding yourself in jeopardy, always adhere to local laws. Stay away from situations where hard drugs are being used, avoid too good to be true scams, show respect to institutions and authorities that legally demand it, and never work here illegally. Be smart, use common sense, and you'll be fine.

EXPAT PERSPECTIVE #5

Backpacker to successful broker

DARREN SHARP
FOUNDER | SEEK2INSURE

www.seek2insure.com

What is your background, and what brought you to Thailand?

Originally from the UK, I moved to Thailand in 2007 after completing my BA in Geography.

Having visited Thailand several times during a backpacking trip in 2004, I felt like Bangkok offered a good mix of opportunity and convenience. I wanted to experience living in the city so moved here straight after graduating.

Whilst I originally only planned to stay for a year and study Thai, I ended up working in Bangkok for a UK based Search Engine Optimisation company called Smart Traffic. Armed with a PC and a phone, I proceeded to build up a portfolio of clients including Toshiba, Thai Airways, and Chubb.

I left Smart Traffic and set up my own SEO company in 2012, which was then acquired by Smart Traffic a year later.

EXPAT PERSPECTIVE

The following year I moved into the health insurance industry and worked for US insurer AETNA. After quickly realising that most brokers were not paying attention to individuals, I went about setting up Seek2Insure. Seek2Insure now works with hundreds of Expats throughout Thailand helping clients find health insurance plans which meet their needs.

What was the biggest surprise or something you didn't expect when you relocated here?

Having spent 9 years living in Bangkok and 6 in Chiang Mai, I now call Phuket home. It never ceases to amaze me as to how much Thailand has to offer. This includes geographically, with amazing nature and landscapes, and culturally with its complex array of subtly different cultures.

What is a bit of wisdom you wish someone had shared with you as you were making Thailand home?

My advice to people wanting to live in Thailand is to go for it. It's absolutely possible to create a successful life here in Thailand. Do not listen to the naysayers! There are always challenges as there are in any country, but with a positive approach Thailand is a great place to overcome challenges.

Thailand is a great place to raise a family. It has great schools, great healthcare, and many things to keep children entertained. From beaches, to mountains, to vibrant cities, Thailand has it all.

Chapter 6:
MAKING
THAILAND HOME

Do you see a future in Thailand?
Deciding on work, home ownership, and staying permanently

As you settle into life in Thailand, it's natural for questions about your future to start surfacing. You may find yourself wondering, "If I'm still interested in working, what should I do about finding a job? Should I buy a home or keep renting? How can I stay permanently without constantly dealing with visas and trips to immigration?" If you've been in Thailand for a while, it's wise to start thinking more strategically about your future here. That's what this chapter is about.

While we'll briefly touch on how to find a job when you arrive, most of this chapter is focused on long-term planning. We'll explore topics like starting a business, buying a house or condo, building a home, and the all important matter of how to legally stay in Thailand forever—whether through permanent residency or citizenship. So if you're ready to start thinking about these bigger decisions, let me give a framework before diving into the particulars.

Thailand, like almost every country, protects the labor force, rewards economic contributions, and reserves certain important rights and privileges to its citizens. There is, for instance, a clear distinction between casually working remotely from Thailand and actively working in the Kingdom or earning income from Thai clients. You can find lots of visa options for remote working, but doing work for a Thai company or generating income within Thailand requires a work permit. If you're caught doing so without one, the penalty is a 99-year ban from the Kingdom.

Thailand offers many incentives for those contributing to the economy, including expats who support Thai families. For instance, folks holding Non-O Marriage visas can obtain a work permit, and the Thai to expat ratio for them is lower than it is for business visa holders. Direct investment, particularly in certain industries, is encouraged by the Board of Investment by allowing foreign ownership, liberal rules on expat staffing, and significant tax benefits. And, as we'll dive into in a bit, working here for three years can be a pathway to truly immigrate and become a permanent resident.

Finally, rights reserved to citizens include the usual ability to vote and participate in the labor force. However, it also includes the right to purchase land. And while you may hear about ways to skirt the law by forming a company, there are many examples of land purchasers facing criminal penalties, even though they were represented by counsel and thought they were covering their bases.

At bottom, unless and until you become a citizen of Thailand, you are a guest in the Kingdom and subject to its laws and legal processes, which may be quite different from what you are accustomed to in your home country. That said, Thailand is historically a welcoming place for anyone who supports the economy, embraces the culture, and patiently follows the rules.

Work and business ownership in Thailand

As mentioned in Chapter 2, Thailand's central location in Southeast Asia makes it an economic hub, and that brings plenty of opportunities for work and business. Of course, that doesn't mean you can have any job you like. To protect the local workforce, the government restricts certain occupations to Thai nationals. Farming and most manual labor, for instance, is off-limits to foreigners. I had a client who owns a painting company and was observed bringing supplies to his crew at a job site. He was just trying to be helpful, but after paying a fine he was careful to always let his crew do the heavy lifting.

Now, as a lawyer based in Bangkok, I am forbidden from practicing Thai law, and I am careful to ensure all legal work here is performed by Thai legal staff. I can manage various aspects of the company as a director, and I practice US immigration law as a member of the California Bar. However, if you engage the firm for a Thai visa or permanent residency, estate planning, and corporate formation, the work will all be performed by a Thai attorney. So you can be a shareholder and director of a company in countless industries, but you need to be thoughtful and understand your permitted ownership stake and role.

Also, as touched on in Chapter 3, your visa plays a role in your ability to get hired as it can come with a Thai-to-foreigner employee ratio requirement. For example, a Non-B visa allows one foreign employee for every four Thai staff. That means if a business has 20 employees, at least 16 must be Thai. If the business owner wants to hire another expat, she'll need to hire four more Thai employees first.

Remember, this ratio varies depending on the visa type. A Marriage visa reduces it to 2:1, while LTR and permanent residency removes the ratio entirely—giving you a notable advantage in the job market.

Despite these restrictions, there are still plenty of opportunities for foreigners who wish to work in Thailand. But if you're new here, you may be wondering how the job market actually works and how to find employment. Let's talk about that.

Finding a job in Thailand

Aside from navigating visa restrictions, finding employment in Thailand is likely similar to what you're accustomed to back home. Job listings are readily available online, including on familiar platforms like LinkedIn and Indeed. You'll also find plenty of local platforms as well, including the popular JobsDB, which is worth a look. There are also professional recruiters and some that specialize in particular industries such as tech and hospitality.

Besides searching for jobs online or throwing your hat in the ring with a recruiter, attending networking events is one of the best ways to make connections and meet decision-makers who could hire you. Bangkok, in particular, has very active chambers of commerce that regularly host networking events attended by business owners and professionals. Some notable chambers include Australia (also the most fun), the UK, the US, and Canada. These chambers typically have monthly wine and dine events where you can mingle with other Westerners, making them great places to make professional connections and new friends. If you're job hunting, attending these events can open unexpected doors.

As with most places, bigger cities offer more employment prospects. Bangkok is undoubtedly the fastest and easiest place to land a job, as there are seemingly countless industries and professional opportunities. Chiang Mai is a good second option. While it's possible to find work in smaller cities like Hua Hin and Koh Samui, the process may take more time and effort compared to the major urban centers.

Remote working

If you are lucky enough to have a remote job and would like to continue it in Thailand, it's important to know only certain visas allow this. Now, if you're here on vacation and need to do a little bit of work and answer emails, it's not a big deal. But if you're staying in Thailand long term and working remotely to earn a living, you need the right visa.

Currently, the three visas that expressly permit remote work in Thailand are the Privilege and LTR visa programs, and the recently introduced DTV visa. Now, while these visas allow you to work for clients and companies located outside of Thailand, earning a salary or revenue from companies based in Thailand requires a work permit issued by the Department of Labor.

Ultimately, remote work can be a fantastic option, especially if you're earning a Western salary and enjoying the cost of living in the Kingdom. If you respect Thai laws and have the right visa in hand, working from Thailand offers an opportunity to more deeply explore Southeast Asia, while putting aside a nice nest egg.

Starting a business

If you want to start a business in Thailand, you have plenty of opportunities—from opening a simple restaurant to building a large marketing agency and countless other ventures. Some expats are incredibly successful here.

That said, when it comes to legally setting up your business, it's important to understand a few key concepts. For instance, almost all business is conducted through Thai limited companies, and with a few exceptions, foreigners are not allowed to hold majority ownership in these entities. Partnerships, limited liability companies, and other business structures just aren't available here.

It is fairly quick and easy to set up a company with the Department of Business Development. Most commonly, expats open their businesses owning 49% of the shares with their Thai partner(s) holding 51%. Of course, this setup comes with risks. Which is why it's crucial that you, as a director, have governance authority and, perhaps more importantly, find a trustworthy Thai partner. In many cases this can be a spouse. It's also important to have a clear and enforceable legal agreement and governance documents in place to protect your interests with, for instance, share buy back rights if things go sideways.

There are opportunities to be a sole or majority shareholder, if you're willing to make the additional investment of time and treasure. For American expats, there is the Treaty of Amity, which allows for 100% foreign ownership of a Thai limited company. This will require a bit more time and paperwork with the Thai government and US Department of Commerce.

For those willing to make a more substantial investment in one of several designated industries, the Thailand Board of Investment (BOI) offers compelling ownership, staffing, and tax incentives designed specifically to attract foreign investment. If your business is included in the BOI's list (it's extensive and available on the BOI's website), you'll need formal BOI approval of your business plan. Think of this as a pitch to an investment bank or private equity firm. There will also be ongoing compliance requirements to assure BOI that your business development is on track. Is it worth the effort? For many owners over the years, the answer has been a resounding yes. So if you're firmly planting a business flag in Thailand, it should be an option that you investigate.

Now, while creating the business entity is straightforward, as someone who owns a business here, I have a few key pieces of advice if you're planning to open shop:

- **Get a good Thai-based accountant on day one:** As a business owner in Thailand, you'll have ongoing Revenue Department, VAT, and social security obligations. It's not uncommon to receive a visit from the Revenue Department or other Thai agencies. A good Thai accountant can help you get everything set up properly, ensure your systems are in order, and check that all of your reporting is complete and up to date. This investment in compliance will pay dividends and give you peace of mind so you can focus on growing your enterprise.

135

- **Find a physical space:** In Thailand, your business needs a physical space, including a space to display your Department of Revenue and other government registrations. That doesn't mean you have to invest in a big office. When getting started, coworking office space facilities work, so long as you have a dedicated address and desk space. You can also carve out space in a private home that is reserved exclusively for the business. And please note that when you go to extend your business visa, you'll need photos of you and your staff in your office space. So plan accordingly.

- **Grow your network:** Lastly, don't underestimate the value of a support network. Owning a business in Thailand can be challenging, especially when navigating the cultural differences that come with managing a Thai staff, negotiating with Thai landlords, or interacting with a variety of Thai government agencies. That's why I highly recommend joining local chambers of commerce or even expat-focused Facebook groups. Here you'll find kindred spirits willing to take business risks and, in many cases, share their experiences.

Opening a business in Thailand isn't something to rush into. Take time to get familiar with your new environment and its culture. Talk to business owners and make some friends. The more grounded and informed you are, the fewer assumptions—and mistakes—you'll make when you're ready to launch your business. I say this from personal experience, having had at least a few unexpected bumps in the road.

Should you own a home, condo, or just rent?

Once you've been in Thailand a while, you may start thinking about buying a home or condo. And why not? If you love living here, it's always nice to have a home base you can call your own. This is especially true if you have a Thai spouse or partner and often stay at the family homestead. Many Thai houses, especially those outside of major cities, aren't designed with Western comforts in mind. They likely lack air conditioning and hot water heaters, have only squat toilets, and you may need a mosquito net for sleeping. Owning your own place or building a house to your specifications (more on this later), can go a long way in making your life in Thailand much more comfortable.

That said, buying a condo or house isn't ever a decision to take lightly. Given the investment, it often only makes sense if you plan to stay in Thailand for the long term and you've firmly committed to the region, town, or neighborhood where you're looking to buy or build in. Now, this is an easier decision if you're relocating to your spouse's home town as I did. And still, there are further considerations before you pour the foundation. Chief among them: foreigners are not allowed to buy land in Thailand. Now, this news is likely to be a bit off putting and contrary to much more liberal ownership rights in your home country. However, there are lawful and common ways for us expats to buy or build a home while feeling secure that it will remain ours for life. So let's dive in.

Condos

Buying a condo anywhere in the country is far more straightforward than purchasing a house. In fact, as an expat, you can be the sole owner and hold the lawful title (called a chanote) to your unit. But wait a second, how is that possible if foreigners can't own land? The key difference is that a condo is part of a larger complex on a shared plot of land. Under well established Thai law, foreigners can legally own up to 49% of a condominium's total unit space, provided that Thai citizens own at least 51%.

Now that you know condo ownership is an option, the next question is, should you buy one? Thailand is, at bottom, a renter's market. New condos are constantly being built, sometimes at a pace that might make you wonder if a housing bubble is on the horizon. The reality is that there's never a shortage of available units (renters, especially Thai nationals, favor the shiny new construction over older units) and rental rates can be remarkably low. Because of this, buying a condo purely as a rental investment is generally not a great financial move.

Does this mean you should never consider buying a condo? Definitely not. If you love a neighborhood in Bangkok or found a place with stunning beach views that will inspire you for years to come, then buying may be the right choice. Ownership also eliminates the risk of being an itinerant renter if your landlord decides not to renew your lease for whatever reason. Plus, many condos in Thailand, especially in major cities, come with excellent amenities like pools, gyms, and rooftop gardens. Having your own condo with a well equipped gym or lap pool can help make Thailand truly feel like home, offering many of the comforts you enjoyed in your home country.

Houses

While purchasing a condo in Thailand is relatively straightforward, buying a house is a bit more complicated. As mentioned earlier, foreigners cannot buy land, but they can buy the house built on it. So how does that work?

You have a couple of options. The first is to purchase only the house itself while leasing the land it sits on. Land leases in Thailand can be as long as 30 years and may provide the option to build a house. While lease renewals are possible, they are not guaranteed. So for this reason, if you choose to move forward with this option, I highly recommend consulting with a Thailand-based property lawyer first.

Another option is if you're married to a Thai. In this scenario, your spouse can buy the property, and the house on top of the land can be jointly owned or you can assume sole ownership. As with the leasing option, there is inherent risk here, particularly if the relationship ends in divorce. Because of this, it may be wise to wait until the relationship has matured, or consult a Thai lawyer and create a prenuptial agreement that clearly defines your rights if the relationship ends.

Also, put a good estate plan in place. You and your family will have greater peace of mind if, for instance, you have the right to live on the property for your lifetime should your spouse predecease you. Your spouse will take comfort if you document your intention to leave your assets, including the house, to your spouse or children. As you've learned in this book, Thai-Western relationships come with challenges. That's why it's critical to ensure a solid, lasting partnership and clearly outline expectations before making big investments.

Building your dream home and avoiding nightmares

I love the house my wife and I have in Phetchabun, and all the planning and effort that went into building it was worth it. There was a vision for indoor/outdoor living spaces, a substantial vegetable garden, and a small caretaker's house so someone was around while Pha and I were on extended visits to the states. It's a home that we both enjoy and rarely leave when I'm not working in Bangkok. Now, like everything else here, the construction process is markedly different from building a house in most Western countries. For that reason, here are a few guidelines and tips if you're considering building your dream home in the Kingdom.

First, invest the time and effort in selecting the right builder. Your fellow expats are happy to share their experiences and nothing beats a solid referral. Even then, take the time to visit properties and projects that the builder has completed or is in the process of constructing. Talk to the owners if you can. Most contractors here are not licensed or bonded, and so your diligence up front is your best insurance for a good outcome.

Next, come up with a design with which the builder and crew are familiar, and try to avoid ploughing new ground. When I first started the process, I engaged a respected architect in Bangkok and added so many design features that no local builder in Phetchabun would touch it. They were concerned about being able to execute the plan and potentially ending up in conflict with us. In the end, we asked to see a portfolio of plans our builder had already completed and found one to our liking. Yes, we changed some dimensions and other details, but when we started breaking ground, both we and our contractor had confidence in the outcome.

Third, be as hands on and present as you can be during the construction process. Builders, and frankly many service providers in Thailand, pride themselves on finding the lowest cost alternative to try and save you some money in the short term. These are good faith efforts borne of satisfying a thrifty clientele. However, when it comes to your home, real value and comfort doesn't equate to the cheapest option. So, feel free to accompany your builder when they're selecting finishes, cabinetry, and appliances. You'll both be happier in the long run.

Finally, treat the crew like family. Having read this far, you know that relationships in Thailand are more personal. If the construction crew is living on site for the build—often away from their families for weeks or months at a time—providing lunch from the local market will be welcomed. And after a long week on the job, sharing a few cold beers and some laughs can be more than just a bit of fun. It will likely lead the crew to treating your new home as if it were their own.

How to stay in Thailand forever: Permanent residency (PR) and citizenship

Once you've sorted out your work and housing, you'll likely find yourself settling into a rhythm. At some point, after returning from an overseas visit or business trip, it may occur to you that you truly feel at home in Thailand. Understand that there are only two ways to truly immigrate to the Kingdom: permanent residency (PR) or Thai citizenship. The good news is that if you work in Thailand for just three years or if you have a Thai spouse and earn a modest salary, it's possible to no longer be a guest of Thailand. With some planning and an investment of time and expense, permanent status is achievable.

The benefits of PR and citizenship

So long as you're staying in Thailand on a visa, your ability to remain depends on circumstances, sometimes outside of your control. Jobs can be lost and family relationships can change. And with these changes of circumstances comes a short time window to figure out an alternative solution, typically just seven days. The primary benefit of PR and citizenship is that you've protected the life you've built in Thailand from unforeseen circumstances.

Beyond a sense of security, PR and citizenship also give you greater freedom of choice. You can change careers, take a break from working, or start your own business without worrying about your visa restricting your choices. PR and citizenship grant you the flexibility to shape your future on your terms, bringing you both peace of mind and long-term stability.

PR

Thailand is much more generous in offering PR to expats compared to many Western countries. In the US, for instance, PR is achievable only through having a spouse or other family relationship, bringing a particular skill set to the table, or making a substantial investment. In Thailand, you qualify for PR if you work in any field, hold the same category of visa for just three years, and earn a modest $2500-3500 salary. If you're married to a Thai and working, the salary requirement is much lower. You'll also need to be able to speak Thai at a basic conversational level.

Now, there are nuances to completing the process and other legal requirements of course. This includes a number of personal records, as well as records and tax filings from your company. There are also documents from your home country you'll need to have certified, including police clearances and educational degrees, so give yourself plenty of time to pull this all together. The PR application window typically opens every October and closes at year's end. Starting the process in the spring or summer is a good idea. It also helps to confer with someone who has been through all of this or engage a trusted representative.

If you qualify, the question many people ask is, "Why now?" After all, there is a substantial investment of both time and money to get your application to the finish line. So like a trip to the dentist or getting your estate plan in place, it's human nature to kick this can down the road. However, I've spoken with too many prospective clients who wish they didn't wait, either due to a job change or looming retirement, and were left scrambling to figure out the best way to continue their lives here. Life throws us curve balls every day, and if you plan to stay in Thailand for the rest of your life, or even a couple decades, PR is the most certain way to ensure you're never uprooted. It also serves as an important step toward obtaining Thai citizenship.

Can you lose PR? Yes, if you fail to return to Thailand at least once during a calendar year (this was all too common during COVID). And you'll oddly need to purchase a multiple re-entry permit every year, something I hope the government reconsiders at some point. And like most countries, you can lose residency status if you violate the law.

Citizenship

For those looking to become an integral part of Thai society, citizenship is the final step in this journey. It grants you all the rights and privileges of Thai nationality, removing every restriction that visa holders and even permanent residents face. As a citizen, you can buy land, own a company outright, work without a permit, and stay in Thailand without any immigration worries.

With this grant of rights and privileges comes responsibility and commitment. Proficiency in the language and knowledge of Thai history, the Royal Family, and civics are required. There is also the time commitment to consider. For instance, you must first be a permanent resident for five years and then complete a lengthy application process that takes an additional three to five years. At the end of this long process, with a Thai identification card and passport in hand, you will truly be home here in the Kingdom. Your baan Thai will have the strongest of all possible foundations.

Final Thoughts

Thank you for taking this journey with me, from tourist to veteran expat, and perhaps to immigrant. As we know well, each of us has different aspirations, perspectives, annoyances, and capabilities. Plotting your unique path when settling into Thailand should be part of the adventure. There is no one right visa, locale, or daily routine that works for everyone.

Two final thoughts. There is a very powerful Buddhist meditation: "I may die today."[11] It's not meant to be a maudlin thought, but rather the expression of a fundamental truth applicable to all sentient beings. So if this was your last day, how would you want to live it? What would you want to express to those you love, and what legacy would you like to leave? It's similar to Rabbi Hillel's question: "If not now, when?"[12] So if perhaps you're considering testing the waters in Thailand or planting your roots more firmly in the Kingdom's soil, why wait?

And finally, the last Buddhist meditation to help you adapt to life in Thailand starts with the premise that you've been reborn over countless lifetimes. As such, everyone you encounter was, over these eons of lifetimes, your mother. Your mother nurtured you when you were helpless and sacrificed her comfort for yours. And for this unconditional love you received from all your mothers over the ages, you feel a deep and abiding compassion for every being you encounter. I know from experience that this is an incredibly difficult thought to keep in mind. But when you are able to do so—especially in Thailand where people often reflect what you are feeling—going about your day with a compassionate heart will be met with smiles, encouragement, and love.

---

[11] I may die today. Geshe Kelsang Gyatso Rinpoche. *THE NEW Meditation Handbook*. Tharpa Publications, 2013.

[12] If not now, when? Hillel the Elder, Mishnah, Pirkei Avot 1:14.

NEED HELP MAKING THAILAND HOME?

Navigating the Thai immigration system can be fraught with legal, cultural, and language challenges. Baan Thai Immigration Solutions strives to be a trusted voice to help expats understand their long-term stay choices and the process of getting to the finish line.

As a strategic advisor, we start with understanding your goals and aspirations, and guide you every step of the way. This best ensures you end up with the ideal visa for your circumstances, so you can stay focused on more important things—like your new life in the Kingdom.

We also provide the most up-to-date information on immigration, corporate and labor policies and regulations, so you can feel confident as you progress in your expat journey.

We can help you with:

- Visas
- Work permits
- Permanent residency
- Opening a business
- Company registration
- BOI registration and compliance

We realize your situation is unique. So if you'd like personalized guidance, contact us today for a free consultation.

Get in touch at hello@btisolutions.co or sign up for a free consultation by completing the form on our Contact page.

Acknowledgements

So many people contributed to this project over the years with their wisdom, experiences, and support. John Weiler was my co-pilot, or more aptly my flight instructor with many wonderful publications under his belt. My gratitude to Scott Pressimone, who planted this seed, and Steve Hazeltine for his insights and edits. Mark Falcioni shot and produced the photographs, and he just happens to put out the best burgers in town (Daniel Thaiger and Stax).

For taking the time to share their hard-earned wisdom and insights, my deep thanks to Ira, Forrest, Jan, Darren, and Joana. Each of their expat perspectives reflects a genuine understanding and compassion for Thailand and are priceless.

My gratitude to the Baan Thai Immigration team runs deep. Our fearless leader Roy and his Thai lawyers Mint, Chub, and Maya. The remarkably talented Pear (classical guitarist), who supports both our Thai and US visa clients. Wil and Martin, who ably help our Thai friends visit or make a new life abroad. And of course, Auy and Cake, without whom the administration of the business would be impossible. A final nod to the heart and soul of Baan Thai, Copter, who was instrumental in the book launch and is also our de facto chief cultural officer.

There are those to whom I owe my career in law. Paul Major, who gave me my first general counsel shot. Susan Liebson, who always displayed patience and kindness. Ron Graves and Howard Schultz, with brand and business building acumen second to none. Michael (MOJ) Johnson and Des Walsh, who had the confidence to allow me to lead a team of legal professionals under challenging circumstances. And Rob Fried, producer of some of the greatest films ever made (*Rudy!*). Special thanks to my first mentors, Doug Berry and Nancy Cohen, who despite busy practices took the time to teach.

Then there are true friends and confidants through the years: Christine and Alan, Malcolm, Michelle and Kevin, David, Julie, Jim, Joe, Eileen, Ahmet, Brad, Cindy, Kim, Ryan, Linda and Chris, Bill, and Mark (and so many others). And for Kru Arissa, who ever so patiently teaches me Thai.

Of course, nothing is possible without the support of family. Meh Joop and Paw Baag, Pope and Bat, who all warmly welcomed me to Ban Phot. Ann and Boy, who share our home and tend our farm with care. My raucous and loving family in New Jersey and Philly, with whom I share so many fond memories.

And then there are our sons, daughters and grand babies, who give me hope for the future: Spike, Annie, Jet, Mew, June, Jessica, Elsie, and Milo. What a blessing.

Finally, Buppha, your patience, partnership, care, and compassion has made all of this possible. Thank you for your partnership and love.

About the Author

Mark resides with his Thai family in Phetchabun Province, Thailand, and leads the Baan Thai Immigration Solutions team from its Bangkok offices. A graduate of the University of Southern California Gould School of Law, he has been a member of the California Bar since 1987. For twenty years, Mark led global legal teams for US privately held and public companies. Today, he serves as the Managing Director of Baan Thai.

A long-time student of Buddhism, Mark has traveled throughout much of SE Asia and India over the past 25 years, drawn not only to the teachings of the region but also its youthful energy and distinctive cuisines.

Mark is an avid reader and drafter of too many legal documents to count. This book marks his first foray into publishing.

www.ingramcontent.com/pod-product-compliance
Lightning Source LLC
Chambersburg PA
CBHW021057130626
46552CB00005B/2140